Texas Notary Horizontal Journal for Notary Signing Agents and Notary Records

by
Brian Greul

Introduction

Thank you for purchasing the Texas Notary Horizontal Journal for Notary Signing Agents and Notary Records. This book has been designed to meet the needs of Texas Notary Signing Agents. It is intended to facilitate efficient, accurate, and detailed notary records, as required by Texas Government Code.

This book is designed to facilitate the typical loan closing with 1 or 2 signers. To assist in making detailed records, each document notarized should be recorded on one line. The fee may be recorded, along with the notarization type(s) and the date of the document. Each signer who the document was notarized for should initial that line. The most common closing documents are pre-printed for convenience. Please see more detailed instructions on pages X and Y.

Should you have suggestions or feedback on ways to improve this book please send email to Books@OcotilloPress.com

---

©2020 Ocotillo Press
ISBN 978-1-954285-02-6

Printed in the United States of America
Second Printing, 2020

Ocotillo Press
5103 Laurel Creek Way
Houston, TX 77017
Books@OcotilloPress.com

Disclaimer: As a Notary Public you are responsible for ensuring that your practice is proper and in compliance. Every attempt has been made to ensure that this record book complies with the requirements of the State of Texas. Nonetheless, the author and publisher disclaim any liability for the content or use of this record book.

Notary Signing Agent (NSA) is a registered trademark of the National Notary Association (NNA) and NNA Services LLC. The NNA is not a sponsor or affiliate of the publisher of this record book and is not a contributor of the content.
For more information on becoming an NSA visit http://nationalnotary.org

This record book belongs to:

Notary Name:	
Notary Address:	
Notary City, State, Zip:	
Notary Residence County:	
Notary Phone:	
Notary Phone:	
Notary Email:	

Record Book Dates of Use:

Date of First Use	Date of Last Use

Notary Commission Information:

State	Commission Number	Commission Expiration

Official Signature:

X_____

Emergency Contact Information:

Emergency Contact 1	Emergency Contact 2

In the event of the death or incapacitation of the Notary this book shall be turned in to the County Clerk Office in the County where the Notary Resides. The Notary's seal shall be destroyed to prevent misuse.

The Texas Secretary of State advises that the Notary shall maintain this journal in a safe place for the longer of the term in which the notarization occurred or 3 years following the date of the notarization. Best practice, however, would be for the notary to permanently maintain copies of the records. (Source: Texas Secretary of State Website)

The NNA recommends a 10 year retention period.

Signer 1 Name and Address: (A)		Signer ... and A
(B)		
Identification ... hod: ☐ Personally Known ☐ Other (C) ☐ Texas Driver... License ☐ Driver's License ☐ Passport	(D)	Identi... ☐ Tex
(E) Sign Here		
X _____	X ____	
Date/Time: (F)	(G) Ref#	
Signing Address: (H)		
Document Date	Notarization	Document Description

A) Name of the Signer
B) Official or claimed address of the signer
C) Checkbox for the type of ID used. If Other note in area D. Credible witness goes in D.
D) expiration date or other data related to ID.
NOTE: Do not record the ID Number or biometric data.
E) Signature (not required in Texas)
F) Date and Time of the Notarization
G) Reference Number
H) Address where Notarization took place if different from official address of signer.

Document Date	Notarization Ack Jur Oth Fee if any	Document Description	Signer Initials	
			1	2
(J)	(K) (I)	Deed of Trust / ...tgage (L)	(M)	(N)
		Deed - Gener... ...it Claim - Special Warranty		
		Borrower's Title Affidavit		

I) Fee, if charged for notarizing this document. Note Texas sets limits on what can be charged for notary services.
J) The date on the document being notarized
K) The type of notarization performed. Acknowledgement, Jurat, Other.
L) The type of document being notarized. Use a blank line to record a document type not listed here. Line through what does not apply.
M/N) After notarization each signer should initial to indicate that the document was notarized.

		(R)		
$				

Notes: (P)

Ack: Do you a... ...ledge this as your signature and your free act and deed, for the purposes stated herein?
Jurat: Do you... (Q) ...nly (swear/affirm) that this statement is true, (so help you God / on your honor)?

P) This area is for recording any notes or comments that relate to the notarization or signing. Deed related information can be recorded here as well to comply with Texas requirements.
Q) Read these aloud for each notarization performed.
R) Blank lines for document types not listed on form.

| Signer 1 Name and Address: | | Signer 2 Name and Address: | |

Identification Method:☐ Personally Known ☐ Other
☐ Texas Driver's License ☐ Driver's License ☐ Passport

Identification Method:☐ Personally Known ☐ Other
☐ Texas Driver's License ☐ Driver's License ☐ Passport

Sign Here

Sign Here

X

X

Date/Time: Ref#:

Signing Address:

Document Date	Notarization **Ack Jur Oth** Fee if any	Document Description	Signer Initials	
			1	2
		Deed of Trust / Mortgage		
		Deed - General - Quit Claim - Special Warranty		
		Borrower's Title Affidavit		
		Borrower's Closing Affidavit		
		E&O / Compliance Agreement		
		Occupancy Affidavit		
		Signature Name Affidavit		
		Power of Attorney - Limited / Durable		
		T-47 Residential Real Property Affidavit		
		Mineral Rights Acknowledgement and Agreement		

	Notes:
Designation of Homestead / Non-Homestead	
Notice of Penalties for Making False or Misleading Statements	
Ownership Affidavit	
Occupancy and Financial Status Affidavit	
Obligation of Debts Affidavit	
Release of Claims and Hold Harmless Agreement	
Affidavit of Marital Status	
Tax Indemnity	
Compliance / Correction Agreement	

9 Ack: Do you acknowledge this as your signature and your free act and deed, for the purposes stated herein?
Jurat: Do you solemnly (swear/affirm) that this statement is true, (so help you God / on your honor)?

| Signer 1 Name and Address: | | Signer 2 Name and Address: | |

Identification Method: ☐ Personally Known ☐ Other
☐ Texas Driver's License ☐ Driver's License ☐ Passport

Identification Method: ☐ Personally Known ☐ Other
☐ Texas Driver's License ☐ Driver's License ☐ Passport

Sign Here

Sign Here

X _____

X _____

Date/Time:

Ref#:

Signing Address:

Document Date	Notarization **Ack Jur Oth** Fee if any	Document Description	Signer Initials	
			1	2
		Deed of Trust / Mortgage		
		Deed - General - Quit Claim - Special Warranty		
		Borrower's Title Affidavit		
		Borrower's Closing Affidavit		
		E&O / Compliance Agreement		
		Occupancy Affidavit		
		Signature Name Affidavit		
		Power of Attorney - Limited / Durable		
		T-47 Residential Real Property Affidavit		
		Mineral Rights Acknowledgement and Agreement		

	Designation of Homestead / Non-Homestead	Notice of Penalties for Making False or Misleading Statements	Ownership Affidavit	Occupancy and Financial Status Affidavit	Obligation of Debts Affidavit	Release of Claims and Hold Harmless Agreement	Affidavit of Marital Status	Tax Indemnity	Compliance / Correction Agreement								

Notes:

11 Ack:Do you acknowledge this as your signature and your free act and deed, for the purposes stated herein?

Jurat: Do you solemnly (swear/affirm) that this statement is true, (so help you God / on your honor)?

Signer 1 Name and Address:		Signer 2 Name and Address:	

Identification Method: ☐ Personally Known ☐ Other ☐ Texas Driver's License ☐ Driver's License ☐ Passport	Identification Method: ☐ Personally Known ☐ Other ☐ Texas Driver's License ☐ Driver's License ☐ Passport

Sign Here

X _____

Sign Here

X _____

Ref # : _____

Date/Time:

Signing Address:

Document Date	Notarization Ack Jur Oth Fee if any	Document Description	Signer Initials	
			1	2
		Deed of Trust / Mortgage		
		Deed - General - Quit Claim - Special Warranty		
		Borrower's Title Affidavit		
		Borrower's Closing Affidavit		
		E&O / Compliance Agreement		
		Occupancy Affidavit		
		Signature Name Affidavit		
		Power of Attorney - Limited / Durable		
		T-47 Residential Real Property Affidavit		
		Mineral Rights Acknowledgement and Agreement		

Document					
Designation of Homestead / Non-Homestead					
Notice of Penalties for Making False or Misleading Statements					
Ownership Affidavit					
Occupancy and Financial Status Affidavit					
Obligation of Debts Affidavit					
Release of Claims and Hold Harmless Agreement					
Affidavit of Marital Status					
Tax Indemnity					
Compliance / Correction Agreement					

Notes:

13 Ack:Do you acknowledge this as your signature and your free act and deed, for the purposes stated herein?
Jurat: Do you solemnly (swear/affirm) that this statement is true, (so help you God / on your honor)?

Signer 1 Name and Address:

Identification Method: ☐ Personally Known   ☐ Other
☐ Texas Driver's License ☐ Driver's License ☐ Passport

X _____

Date/Time: _____

Signing Address:

Signer 2 Name and Address:

Identification Method: ☐ Personally Known   ☐ Other
☐ Texas Driver's License ☐ Driver's License ☐ Passport

X _____

Ref #: _____

Document Date	Notarization Ack Jur Oth Fee if any	Document Description	Signer Initials 1	2
		Deed of Trust / Mortgage		
		Deed - General - Quit Claim - Special Warranty		
		Borrower's Title Affidavit		
		Borrower's Closing Affidavit		
		E&O / Compliance Agreement		
		Occupancy Affidavit		
		Signature Name Affidavit		
		Power of Attorney - Limited / Durable		
		T-47 Residential Real Property Affidavit		
		Mineral Rights Acknowledgement and Agreement		

Designation of Homestead / Non-Homestead															
Notice of Penalties for Making False or Misleading Statements															
Ownership Affidavit															
Occupancy and Financial Status Affidavit															
Obligation of Debts Affidavit															
Release of Claims and Hold Harmless Agreement															
Affidavit of Marital Status															
Tax Indemnity															
Compliance / Correction Agreement															

Notes:

15 Ack: Do you acknowledge this as your signature and your free act and deed, for the purposes stated herein?
Jurat: Do you solemnly (swear/affirm) that this statement is true, (so help you God / on your honor)?

| Signer 1 Name and Address: | | Signer 2 Name and Address: | |

Identification Method: ☐ Personally Known ☐ Other
☐ Texas Driver's License ☐ Driver's License ☐ Passport

Identification Method: ☐ Personally Known ☐ Other
☐ Texas Driver's License ☐ Driver's License ☐ Passport

Sign Here

Sign Here

X _____

X _____

Date/Time:

Ref#:

Signing Address:

Document Date	Notarization Ack **J**ur **O**th Fee if any	Document Description	Signer Initials	
			1	2
		Deed of Trust / Mortgage		
		Deed - General - Quit Claim - Special Warranty		
		Borrower's Title Affidavit		
		Borrower's Closing Affidavit		
		E&O / Compliance Agreement		
		Occupancy Affidavit		
		Signature Name Affidavit		
		Power of Attorney - Limited / Durable		
		T-47 Residential Real Property Affidavit		
		Mineral Rights Acknowledgement and Agreement		

Designation of Homestead / Non-Homestead	
Notice of Penalties for Making False or Misleading Statements	
Ownership Affidavit	
Occupancy and Financial Status Affidavit	
Obligation of Debts Affidavit	
Release of Claims and Hold Harmless Agreement	
Affidavit of Marital Status	
Tax Indemnity	
Compliance / Correction Agreement	

Notes:

Ack: Do you acknowledge this as your signature and your free act and deed, for the purposes stated herein?

Jurat: Do you solemnly (swear/affirm) that this statement is true, (so help you God / on your honor)?

17

Signer 1 Name
and Address:

Signer 2 Name
and Address:

Identification Method: □ Personally Known   □ Other
□ Texas Driver's License □ Driver's License □ Passport

Identification Method: □ Personally Known   □ Other
□ Texas Driver's License □ Driver's License □ Passport

Sign Here

Sign Here

X _____

X _____

Date/Time:

Ref #:

Signing Address:

Document Date	Notarization Ack **Jur O**th Fee if any	Document Description	Signer Initials	
			1	2
		Deed of Trust / Mortgage		
		Deed - General - Quit Claim - Special Warranty		
		Borrower's Title Affidavit		
		Borrower's Closing Affidavit		
		E&O / Compliance Agreement		
		Occupancy Affidavit		
		Signature Name Affidavit		
		Power of Attorney - Limited / Durable		
		T-47 Residential Real Property Affidavit		
		Mineral Rights Acknowledgement and Agreement		

	Designation of Homestead / Non-Homestead
	Notice of Penalties for Making False or Misleading Statements
	Ownership Affidavit
	Occupancy and Financial Status Affidavit
	Obligation of Debts Affidavit
	Release of Claims and Hold Harmless Agreement
	Affidavit of Marital Status
	Tax Indemnity
	Compliance / Correction Agreement

Notes:

Ack: Do you acknowledge this as your signature and your free act and deed, for the purposes stated herein?

Jurat: Do you solemnly (swear/affirm) that this statement is true, (so help you God / on your honor)?

Signer 1 Name and Address:		Signer 2 Name and Address:	
Identification Method: ☐ Personally Known ☐ Other ☐ Texas Driver's License ☐ Driver's License ☐ Passport		Identification Method: ☐ Personally Known ☐ Other ☐ Texas Driver's License ☐ Driver's License ☐ Passport	

Sign Here

X _____

Sign Here

X _____

Date/Time: _____   Ref #: _____

Signing Address: _____

Document Date	Notarization **Ack Jur Oth** Fee if any	Document Description	Signer Initials	
			1	2
		Deed of Trust / Mortgage		
		Deed - General - Quit Claim - Special Warranty		
		Borrower's Title Affidavit		
		Borrower's Closing Affidavit		
		E&O / Compliance Agreement		
		Occupancy Affidavit		
		Signature Name Affidavit		
		Power of Attorney - Limited / Durable		
		T-47 Residential Real Property Affidavit		
		Mineral Rights Acknowledgement and Agreement		

Designation of Homestead / Non-Homestead	Notice of Penalties for Making False or Misleading Statements	Ownership Affidavit	Occupancy and Financial Status Affidavit	Obligation of Debts Affidavit	Release of Claims and Hold Harmless Agreement	Affidavit of Marital Status	Tax Indemnity	Compliance / Correction Agreement							

Notes:

21

Ack: Do you acknowledge this as your signature and your free act and deed, for the purposes stated herein?

Jurat: Do you solemnly (swear/affirm) that this statement is true, (so help you God / on your honor)?

| Signer 1 Name and Address: | | Signer 2 Name and Address: | |

Identification Method: ☐ Personally Known ☐ Other
☐ Texas Driver's License ☐ Driver's License ☐ Passport

Identification Method: ☐ Personally Known ☐ Other
☐ Texas Driver's License ☐ Driver's License ☐ Passport

Sign Here

Sign Here

X _____

X _____

Date/Time:

Ref#:

Signing Address:

Document Date	Notarization Ack Jur Oth Fee if any	Document Description	Signer Initials 1	2
		Deed of Trust / Mortgage		
		Deed - General - Quit Claim - Special Warranty		
		Borrower's Title Affidavit		
		Borrower's Closing Affidavit		
		E&O / Compliance Agreement		
		Occupancy Affidavit		
		Signature Name Affidavit		
		Power of Attorney - Limited / Durable		
		T-47 Residential Real Property Affidavit		
		Mineral Rights Acknowledgement and Agreement		

		Designation of Homestead / Non-Homestead
		Notice of Penalties for Making False or Misleading Statements
		Ownership Affidavit
		Occupancy and Financial Status Affidavit
		Obligation of Debts Affidavit
		Release of Claims and Hold Harmless Agreement
		Affidavit of Marital Status
		Tax Indemnity
		Compliance / Correction Agreement

Notes:

23 Ack: Do you acknowledge this as your signature and your free act and deed, for the purposes stated herein?
Jurat: Do you solemnly (swear/affirm) that this statement is true, (so help you God / on your honor)?

Signer 1 Name
and Address:

Signer 2 Name
and Address:

Identification Method: ☐ Personally Known ☐ Other
☐ Texas Driver's License ☐ Driver's License ☐ Passport

Identification Method: ☐ Personally Known ☐ Other
☐ Texas Driver's License ☐ Driver's License ☐ Passport

Sign Here

Sign Here

X _____

X _____

Date/Time: _____   Ref#: _____

Signing Address: _____

Document Date	Notarization Ack **Jur** **Oth** Fee if any	Document Description	Signer Initials	
			1	2
		Deed of Trust / Mortgage		
		Deed - General - Quit Claim - Special Warranty		
		Borrower's Title Affidavit		
		Borrower's Closing Affidavit		
		E&O / Compliance Agreement		
		Occupancy Affidavit		
		Signature Name Affidavit		
		Power of Attorney - Limited / Durable		
		T-47 Residential Real Property Affidavit		
		Mineral Rights Acknowledgement and Agreement		

	Designation of Homestead / Non-Homestead	Notice of Penalties for Making False or Misleading Statements	Ownership Affidavit	Occupancy and Financial Status Affidavit	Obligation of Debts Affidavit	Release of Claims and Hold Harmless Agreement	Affidavit of Marital Status	Tax Indemnity	Compliance / Correction Agreement						

Notes:

Ack: Do you acknowledge this as your signature and your free act and deed, for the purposes stated herein?
Jurat: Do you solemnly (swear/affirm) that this statement is true, (so help you God / on your honor)?

Signer 1 Name and Address:		Signer 2 Name and Address:	
Identification Method: ☐ Personally Known ☐ Other ☐ Texas Driver's License ☐ Driver's License ☐ Passport		Identification Method: ☐ Personally Known ☐ Other ☐ Texas Driver's License ☐ Driver's License ☐ Passport	

Sign Here

X _____

Sign Here

X _____

Date/Time:

Ref #:

Signing Address:

Document Date	Notarization **A**ck **J**ur **O**th Fee if any	Document Description	Signer Initials	
			1	2
		Deed of Trust / Mortgage		
		Deed – General – Quit Claim – Special Warranty		
		Borrower's Title Affidavit		
		Borrower's Closing Affidavit		
		E&O / Compliance Agreement		
		Occupancy Affidavit		
		Signature Name Affidavit		
		Power of Attorney – Limited / Durable		
		T-47 Residential Real Property Affidavit		
		Mineral Rights Acknowledgement and Agreement		

	Designation of Homestead / Non-Homestead
	Notice of Penalties for Making False or Misleading Statements
	Ownership Affidavit
	Occupancy and Financial Status Affidavit
	Obligation of Debts Affidavit
	Release of Claims and Hold Harmless Agreement
	Affidavit of Marital Status
	Tax Indemnity
	Compliance / Correction Agreement

Notes:

27 Ack: Do you acknowledge this as your signature and your free act and deed, for the purposes stated herein?
Jurat: Do you solemnly (swear/affirm) that this statement is true, (so help you God / on your honor)?

Signer 1 Name
and Address:

Signer 2 Name
and Address:

Identification Method:☐ Personally Known   ☐ Other
☐ Texas Driver's License ☐ Driver's License ☐ Passport

Identification Method:☐ Personally Known   ☐ Other
☐ Texas Driver's License ☐ Driver's License ☐ Passport

Sign Here

Sign Here

X _____

X _____

Date/Time: Ref#:

Signing Address:

Document Date	Notarization Ack Jur Oth Fee if any	Document Description	Signer Initials	
			1	2
		Deed of Trust / Mortgage		
		Deed - General - Quit Claim - Special Warranty		
		Borrower's Title Affidavit		
		Borrower's Closing Affidavit		
		E&O / Compliance Agreement		
		Occupancy Affidavit		
		Signature Name Affidavit		
		Power of Attorney - Limited / Durable		
		T-47 Residential Real Property Affidavit		
		Mineral Rights Acknowledgement and Agreement		

		Designation of Homestead / Non-Homestead
		Notice of Penalties for Making False or Misleading Statements
		Ownership Affidavit
		Occupancy and Financial Status Affidavit
		Obligation of Debts Affidavit
		Release of Claims and Hold Harmless Agreement
		Affidavit of Marital Status
		Tax Indemnity
		Compliance / Correction Agreement

Notes:

29 Ack:Do you acknowledge this as your signature and your free act and deed, for the purposes stated herein?
Jurat: Do you solemnly (swear/affirm) that this statement is true, (so help you God / on your honor)?

Signer 1 Name and Address:

Signer 2 Name and Address:

Identification Method: ☐ Personally Known ☐ Other
☐ Texas Driver's License ☐ Driver's License ☐ Passport

Identification Method: ☐ Personally Known ☐ Other
☐ Texas Driver's License ☐ Driver's License ☐ Passport

Sign Here

X _____

Sign Here

X _____

Date/Time: _____   Ref#: _____

Signing Address:

Document Date	Notarization Ack **J**ur **O**th Fee if any	Document Description	Signer Initials	
			1	2
		Deed of Trust / Mortgage		
		Deed - General - Quit Claim - Special Warranty		
		Borrower's Title Affidavit		
		Borrower's Closing Affidavit		
		E&O / Compliance Agreement		
		Occupancy Affidavit		
		Signature Name Affidavit		
		Power of Attorney - Limited / Durable		
		T-47 Residential Real Property Affidavit		
		Mineral Rights Acknowledgement and Agreement		

	Designation of Homestead / Non-Homestead
	Notice of Penalties for Making False or Misleading Statements
	Ownership Affidavit
	Occupancy and Financial Status Affidavit
	Obligation of Debts Affidavit
	Release of Claims and Hold Harmless Agreement
	Affidavit of Marital Status
	Tax Indemnity
	Compliance / Correction Agreement

Notes:

Ack: Do you acknowledge this as your signature and your free act and deed, for the purposes stated herein?
Jurat: Do you solemnly (swear/affirm) that this statement is true, (so help you God / on your honor)?

Signer 1 Name
and Address:

Signer 2 Name
and Address:

Identification Method: ☐ Personally Known   ☐ Other
☐ Texas Driver's License ☐ Driver's License ☐ Passport

Identification Method: ☐ Personally Known   ☐ Other
☐ Texas Driver's License ☐ Driver's License ☐ Passport

Sign Here

Sign Here

X _____

X _____

Date/Time:

Ref#:

Signing Address:

Document Date	Notarization Ack **Jur** O**th** Fee if any	Document Description	Signer Initials	
			1	2
		Deed of Trust / Mortgage		
		Deed - General - Quit Claim - Special Warranty		
		Borrower's Title Affidavit		
		Borrower's Closing Affidavit		
		E&O / Compliance Agreement		
		Occupancy Affidavit		
		Signature Name Affidavit		
		Power of Attorney - Limited / Durable		
		T-47 Residential Real Property Affidavit		
		Mineral Rights Acknowledgement and Agreement		

		Designation of Homestead / Non-Homestead													
		Notice of Penalties for Making False or Misleading Statements													
		Ownership Affidavit													
		Occupancy and Financial Status Affidavit													
		Obligation of Debts Affidavit													
		Release of Claims and Hold Harmless Agreement													
		Affidavit of Marital Status													
		Tax Indemnity													
		Compliance / Correction Agreement													

Notes:

33   Ack: Do you acknowledge this as your signature and your free act and deed, for the purposes stated herein?
Jurat: Do you solemnly (swear/affirm) that this statement is true, (so help you God / on your honor)?

| Signer 1 Name and Address: | | Signer 2 Name and Address: | |

Identification Method: ☐ Personally Known ☐ Other
☐ Texas Driver's License ☐ Driver's License ☐ Passport

Identification Method: ☐ Personally Known ☐ Other
☐ Texas Driver's License ☐ Driver's License ☐ Passport

Sign Here

Sign Here

X _____

X _____

Date/Time:

Ref#:

Signing Address:

Document Date	Notarization Ack **J**ur **O**th Fee if any	Document Description	Signer Initials	
			1	2
		Deed of Trust / Mortgage		
		Deed - General - Quit Claim - Special Warranty		
		Borrower's Title Affidavit		
		Borrower's Closing Affidavit		
		E&O / Compliance Agreement		
		Occupancy Affidavit		
		Signature Name Affidavit		
		Power of Attorney - Limited / Durable		
		T-47 Residential Real Property Affidavit		
		Mineral Rights Acknowledgement and Agreement		

	Designation of Homestead / Non-Homestead
	Notice of Penalties for Making False or Misleading Statements
	Ownership Affidavit
	Occupancy and Financial Status Affidavit
	Obligation of Debts Affidavit
	Release of Claims and Hold Harmless Agreement
	Affidavit of Marital Status
	Tax Indemnity
	Compliance / Correction Agreement

Notes:

35 Ack: Do you acknowledge this as your signature and your free act and deed, for the purposes stated herein?
Jurat: Do you solemnly (swear/affirm) that this statement is true, (so help you God / on your honor)?

Signer 1 Name
and Address:

Signer 2 Name
and Address:

Identification Method: ☐ Personally Known   ☐ Other
☐ Texas Driver's License ☐ Driver's License ☐ Passport

Identification Method: ☐ Personally Known   ☐ Other
☐ Texas Driver's License ☐ Driver's License ☐ Passport

Sign Here

Sign Here

X _____

X _____

Date/Time: _____   Ref#: _____

Signing Address:

Document Date	Notarization Ack Jur Oth Fee if any	Document Description	Signer Initials	
			1	2
		Deed of Trust / Mortgage		
		Deed - General - Quit Claim - Special Warranty		
		Borrower's Title Affidavit		
		Borrower's Closing Affidavit		
		E&O / Compliance Agreement		
		Occupancy Affidavit		
		Signature Name Affidavit		
		Power of Attorney - Limited / Durable		
		T-47 Residential Real Property Affidavit		
		Mineral Rights Acknowledgement and Agreement		

			Designation of Homestead / Non-Homestead
			Notice of Penalties for Making False or Misleading Statements
			Ownership Affidavit
			Occupancy and Financial Status Affidavit
			Obligation of Debts Affidavit
			Release of Claims and Hold Harmless Agreement
			Affidavit of Marital Status
			Tax Indemnity
			Compliance / Correction Agreement

Notes:

37 Ack: Do you acknowledge this as your signature and your free act and deed, for the purposes stated herein?
Jurat: Do you solemnly (swear/affirm) that this statement is true, (so help you God / on your honor)?

Signer 1 Name and Address:		Signer 2 Name and Address:	

Identification Method: ☐ Personally Known   ☐ Other
☐ Texas Driver's License   ☐ Driver's License   ☐ Passport

Identification Method: ☐ Personally Known   ☐ Other
☐ Texas Driver's License   ☐ Driver's License   ☐ Passport

Sign Here

Sign Here

X _____   X _____

Date/Time: _____   **Ref#:** _____

Signing Address:

Document Date	Notarization Ack Jur Oth Fee if any	Document Description	Signer Initials	
			1	2
		Deed of Trust / Mortgage		
		Deed - General - Quit Claim - Special Warranty		
		Borrower's Title Affidavit		
		Borrower's Closing Affidavit		
		E&O / Compliance Agreement		
		Occupancy Affidavit		
		Signature Name Affidavit		
		Power of Attorney - Limited / Durable		
		T-47 Residential Real Property Affidavit		
		Mineral Rights Acknowledgement and Agreement		

	Designation of Homestead / Non-Homestead	Notice of Penalties for Making False or Misleading Statements	Ownership Affidavit	Occupancy and Financial Status Affidavit	Obligation of Debts Affidavit	Release of Claims and Hold Harmless Agreement	Affidavit of Marital Status	Tax Indemnity	Compliance / Correction Agreement					

Notes:

Ack:Do you acknowledge this as your signature and your free act and deed, for the purposes stated herein?
Jurat: Do you solemnly (swear/affirm) that this statement is true, (so help you God / on your honor)?

Signer 1 Name
and Address:

Signer 2 Name
and Address:

Identification Method:☐ Personally Known ☐ Other
☐ Texas Driver's License ☐ Driver's License ☐ Passport

Identification Method:☐ Personally Known ☐ Other
☐ Texas Driver's License ☐ Driver's License ☐ Passport

Sign Here

Sign Here

X _____

X _____

Date/Time: _____   Ref#: _____

Signing Address:

Document Date	Notarization Ack **J**ur **O**th Fee if any	Document Description	Signer Initials	
			1	2
		Deed of Trust / Mortgage		
		Deed - General - Quit Claim - Special Warranty		
		Borrower's Title Affidavit		
		Borrower's Closing Affidavit		
		E&O / Compliance Agreement		
		Occupancy Affidavit		
		Signature Name Affidavit		
		Power of Attorney - Limited / Durable		
		T-47 Residential Real Property Affidavit		
		Mineral Rights Acknowledgement and Agreement		

Designation of Homestead / Non-Homestead		
Notice of Penalties for Making False or Misleading Statements		
Ownership Affidavit		
Occupancy and Financial Status Affidavit		
Obligation of Debts Affidavit		
Release of Claims and Hold Harmless Agreement		
Affidavit of Marital Status		
Tax Indemnity		
Compliance / Correction Agreement		

Notes:

41 Ack:Do you acknowledge this as your signature and your free act and deed, for the purposes stated herein?
Jurat: Do you solemnly (swear/affirm) that this statement is true, (so help you God / on your honor)?

| Signer 1 Name and Address: | | Signer 2 Name and Address: | |

Signer 1 Name and Address:

Signer 2 Name and Address:

Identification Method: ☐ Personally Known ☐ Other
☐ Texas Driver's License ☐ Driver's License ☐ Passport

Identification Method: ☐ Personally Known ☐ Other
☐ Texas Driver's License ☐ Driver's License ☐ Passport

Sign Here

Sign Here

X _____

X _____

Ref#: _____

Date/Time:

Signing Address:

Document Date	Notarization Ack **J**ur **O**th Fee if any	Document Description	Signer Initials	
			1	2
		Deed of Trust / Mortgage		
		Deed - General - Quit Claim - Special Warranty		
		Borrower's Title Affidavit		
		Borrower's Closing Affidavit		
		E&O / Compliance Agreement		
		Occupancy Affidavit		
		Signature Name Affidavit		
		Power of Attorney - Limited / Durable		
		T-47 Residential Real Property Affidavit		
		Mineral Rights Acknowledgement and Agreement		

Designation of Homestead / Non-Homestead	
Notice of Penalties for Making False or Misleading Statements	
Ownership Affidavit	
Occupancy and Financial Status Affidavit	
Obligation of Debts Affidavit	
Release of Claims and Hold Harmless Agreement	
Affidavit of Marital Status	
Tax Indemnity	
Compliance / Correction Agreement	

Notes:

43 Ack: Do you acknowledge this as your signature and your free act and deed, for the purposes stated herein?
Jurat: Do you solemnly (swear/affirm) that this statement is true, (so help you God / on your honor)?

| Signer 1 Name and Address: | | Signer 2 Name and Address: | |

Identification Method: ☐ Personally Known ☐ Other
☐ Texas Driver's License ☐ Driver's License ☐ Passport

Identification Method: ☐ Personally Known ☐ Other
☐ Texas Driver's License ☐ Driver's License ☐ Passport

Sign Here   Sign Here

X _____ X _____

Date/Time: _____   **Ref#:** _____

Signing Address:

Document Date	Notarization **A**ck **J**ur **O**th Fee if any	Document Description	Signer Initials	
			1	2
		Deed of Trust / Mortgage		
		Deed - General - Quit Claim - Special Warranty		
		Borrower's Title Affidavit		
		Borrower's Closing Affidavit		
		E&O / Compliance Agreement		
		Occupancy Affidavit		
		Signature Name Affidavit		
		Power of Attorney - Limited / Durable		
		T-47 Residential Real Property Affidavit		
		Mineral Rights Acknowledgement and Agreement		

Designation of Homestead / Non-Homestead		
Notice of Penalties for Making False or Misleading Statements		
Ownership Affidavit		
Occupancy and Financial Status Affidavit		
Obligation of Debts Affidavit		
Release of Claims and Hold Harmless Agreement		
Affidavit of Marital Status		
Tax Indemnity		
Compliance / Correction Agreement		

Notes:

45 Ack: Do you acknowledge this as your signature and your free act and deed, for the purposes stated herein?
Jurat: Do you solemnly (swear/affirm) that this statement is true, (so help you God / on your honor)?

Signer 1 Name and Address:		Signer 2 Name and Address:

Identification Method: ☐ Personally Known ☐ Other ☐ Texas Driver's License ☐ Driver's License ☐ Passport	Identification Method: ☐ Personally Known ☐ Other ☐ Texas Driver's License ☐ Driver's License ☐ Passport

Sign Here

Sign Here

X _____   X _____

Date/Time: _____   Ref#: _____

Signing Address: _____

Document Date	Notarization Ack **Jur O**th Fee if any	Document Description	Signer Initials	
			1	2
		Deed of Trust / Mortgage		
		Deed - General - Quit Claim - Special Warranty		
		Borrower's Title Affidavit		
		Borrower's Closing Affidavit		
		E&O / Compliance Agreement		
		Occupancy Affidavit		
		Signature Name Affidavit		
		Power of Attorney - Limited / Durable		
		T-47 Residential Real Property Affidavit		
		Mineral Rights Acknowledgement and Agreement		

Designation of Homestead / Non-Homestead			
Notice of Penalties for Making False or Misleading Statements			
Ownership Affidavit			
Occupancy and Financial Status Affidavit			
Obligation of Debts Affidavit			
Release of Claims and Hold Harmless Agreement			
Affidavit of Marital Status			
Tax Indemnity			
Compliance / Correction Agreement			

Notes:

47 Ack:Do you acknowledge this as your signature and your free act and deed, for the purposes stated herein?
Jurat: Do you solemnly (swear/affirm) that this statement is true, (so help you God / on your honor)?

Signer 1 Name and Address:		Signer 2 Name and Address:	

Identification Method: ☐ Personally Known ☐ Other
☐ Texas Driver's License ☐ Driver's License ☐ Passport

Identification Method: ☐ Personally Known ☐ Other
☐ Texas Driver's License ☐ Driver's License ☐ Passport

Sign Here

Sign Here

X _____

X _____ Ref#: _____

Date/Time: _____

Signing Address: _____

Document Date	Notarization Ack Jur Oth Fee if any	Document Description	Signer Initials	
			1	2
		Deed of Trust / Mortgage		
		Deed - General - Quit Claim - Special Warranty		
		Borrower's Title Affidavit		
		Borrower's Closing Affidavit		
		E&O / Compliance Agreement		
		Occupancy Affidavit		
		Signature Name Affidavit		
		Power of Attorney - Limited / Durable		
		T-47 Residential Real Property Affidavit		
		Mineral Rights Acknowledgement and Agreement		

			Designation of Homestead / Non-Homestead												
			Notice of Penalties for Making False or Misleading Statements												
			Ownership Affidavit												
			Occupancy and Financial Status Affidavit												
			Obligation of Debts Affidavit												
			Release of Claims and Hold Harmless Agreement												
			Affidavit of Marital Status												
			Tax Indemnity												
			Compliance / Correction Agreement												

Notes:

Ack:Do you acknowledge this as your signature and your free act and deed, for the purposes stated herein?

Jurat: Do you solemnly (swear/affirm) that this statement is true, (so help you God / on your honor)?

49

| Signer 1 Name and Address: | | Signer 2 Name and Address: | |

Signer 1 Name and Address:

Signer 2 Name and Address:

Identification Method: □ Personally Known □ Other
□ Texas Driver's License □ Driver's License □ Passport

Identification Method: □ Personally Known □ Other
□ Texas Driver's License □ Driver's License □ Passport

Sign Here

Sign Here

X _____

X _____

Date/Time:

Ref #:

Signing Address:

Document Date	Notarization Ack Jur Oth Fee if any	Document Description	Signer Initials	
			1	2
		Deed of Trust / Mortgage		
		Deed - General - Quit Claim - Special Warranty		
		Borrower's Title Affidavit		
		Borrower's Closing Affidavit		
		E&O / Compliance Agreement		
		Occupancy Affidavit		
		Signature Name Affidavit		
		Power of Attorney - Limited / Durable		
		T-47 Residential Real Property Affidavit		
		Mineral Rights Acknowledgement and Agreement		

	Designation of Homestead / Non-Homestead	Notice of Penalties for Making False or Misleading Statements	Ownership Affidavit	Occupancy and Financial Status Affidavit	Obligation of Debts Affidavit	Release of Claims and Hold Harmless Agreement	Affidavit of Marital Status	Tax Indemnity	Compliance / Correction Agreement								

Notes:

Ack: Do you acknowledge this as your signature and your free act and deed, for the purposes stated herein?
Jurat: Do you solemnly (swear/affirm) that this statement is true, (so help you God / on your honor)?

Signer 1 Name and Address:		Signer 2 Name and Address:	

Identification Method: ☐ Personally Known ☐ Other ☐ Texas Driver's License ☐ Driver's License ☐ Passport	Identification Method: ☐ Personally Known ☐ Other ☐ Texas Driver's License ☐ Driver's License ☐ Passport

Sign Here

X _____   X _____   Ref #:

Date/Time:

Signing Address:

Document Date	Notarization **A**ck **J**ur **O**th Fee if any	Document Description	Signer Initials	
			1	2
		Deed of Trust / Mortgage		
		Deed – General – Quit Claim – Special Warranty		
		Borrower's Title Affidavit		
		Borrower's Closing Affidavit		
		E&O / Compliance Agreement		
		Occupancy Affidavit		
		Signature Name Affidavit		
		Power of Attorney – Limited / Durable		
		T-47 Residential Real Property Affidavit		
		Mineral Rights Acknowledgement and Agreement		

		Designation of Homestead / Non-Homestead		
		Notice of Penalties for Making False or Misleading Statements		
		Ownership Affidavit		
		Occupancy and Financial Status Affidavit		
		Obligation of Debts Affidavit		
		Release of Claims and Hold Harmless Agreement		
		Affidavit of Marital Status		
		Tax Indemnity		
		Compliance / Correction Agreement		

Notes:

53 Ack:Do you acknowledge this as your signature and your free act and deed, for the purposes stated herein?
Jurat: Do you solemnly (swear/affirm) that this statement is true, (so help you God / on your honor)?

Signer 1 Name and Address:		Signer 2 Name and Address:	

Identification Method: ☐ Personally Known ☐ Other
☐ Texas Driver's License ☐ Driver's License ☐ Passport

Identification Method: ☐ Personally Known ☐ Other
☐ Texas Driver's License ☐ Driver's License ☐ Passport

Sign Here

X _____

Sign Here

X _____

Date/Time: _____   Ref#: _____

Signing Address: _____

Document Date	Notarization Ack Jur Oth Fee if any	Document Description	Signer Initials	
			1	2
		Deed of Trust / Mortgage		
		Deed - General - Quit Claim - Special Warranty		
		Borrower's Title Affidavit		
		Borrower's Closing Affidavit		
		E&O / Compliance Agreement		
		Occupancy Affidavit		
		Signature Name Affidavit		
		Power of Attorney - Limited / Durable		
		T-47 Residential Real Property Affidavit		
		Mineral Rights Acknowledgement and Agreement		

			Designation of Homestead / Non-Homestead
			Notice of Penalties for Making False or Misleading Statements
			Ownership Affidavit
			Occupancy and Financial Status Affidavit
			Obligation of Debts Affidavit
			Release of Claims and Hold Harmless Agreement
			Affidavit of Marital Status
			Tax Indemnity
			Compliance / Correction Agreement

Notes:

Ack: Do you acknowledge this as your signature and your free act and deed, for the purposes stated herein?

Jurat: Do you solemnly (swear/affirm) that this statement is true, (so help you God / on your honor)?

55

| Signer 1 Name and Address: | | Signer 2 Name and Address: | |

Identification Method: ☐ Personally Known ☐ Other
☐ Texas Driver's License ☐ Driver's License ☐ Passport

Identification Method: ☐ Personally Known ☐ Other
☐ Texas Driver's License ☐ Driver's License ☐ Passport

Sign Here

Sign Here

X _____ X _____

Date/Time: _____ Ref #: _____

Signing Address:

Document Date	Notarization Ack **J**ur **O**th Fee if any	Document Description	Signer Initials	
			1	2
		Deed of Trust / Mortgage		
		Deed - General - Quit Claim - Special Warranty		
		Borrower's Title Affidavit		
		Borrower's Closing Affidavit		
		E&O / Compliance Agreement		
		Occupancy Affidavit		
		Signature Name Affidavit		
		Power of Attorney - Limited / Durable		
		T-47 Residential Real Property Affidavit		
		Mineral Rights Acknowledgement and Agreement		

	Designation of Homestead / Non-Homestead	Notice of Penalties for Making False or Misleading Statements	Ownership Affidavit	Occupancy and Financial Status Affidavit	Obligation of Debts Affidavit	Release of Claims and Hold Harmless Agreement	Affidavit of Marital Status	Tax Indemnity	Compliance / Correction Agreement								

Notes:

57 Ack: Do you acknowledge this as your signature and your free act and deed, for the purposes stated herein?
Jurat: Do you solemnly (swear/affirm) that this statement is true, (so help you God / on your honor)?

Signer 1 Name and Address:

Signer 2 Name and Address:

Identification Method: □ Personally Known □ Other
□ Texas Driver's License □ Driver's License □ Passport

Identification Method: □ Personally Known □ Other
□ Texas Driver's License □ Driver's License □ Passport

Sign Here

Sign Here

X _____

X _____

Date/Time:

Ref#:

Signing Address:

Document Date	Notarization Ack Jur Oth Fee if any	Document Description	Signer Initials	
			1	2
		Deed of Trust / Mortgage		
		Deed - General - Quit Claim - Special Warranty		
		Borrower's Title Affidavit		
		Borrower's Closing Affidavit		
		E&O / Compliance Agreement		
		Occupancy Affidavit		
		Signature Name Affidavit		
		Power of Attorney - Limited / Durable		
		T-47 Residential Real Property Affidavit		
		Mineral Rights Acknowledgement and Agreement		

Document		
Designation of Homestead / Non-Homestead		
Notice of Penalties for Making False or Misleading Statements		
Ownership Affidavit		
Occupancy and Financial Status Affidavit		
Obligation of Debts Affidavit		
Release of Claims and Hold Harmless Agreement		
Affidavit of Marital Status		
Tax Indemnity		
Compliance / Correction Agreement		

Notes:

59 Ack:Do you acknowledge this as your signature and your free act and deed, for the purposes stated herein?
Jurat: Do you solemnly (swear/affirm) that this statement is true, (so help you God / on your honor)?

Signer 1 Name and Address:		Signer 2 Name and Address:	
Identification Method: ☐ Personally Known ☐ Other ☐ Texas Driver's License ☐ Driver's License ☐ Passport		Identification Method: ☐ Personally Known ☐ Other ☐ Texas Driver's License ☐ Driver's License ☐ Passport	

Sign Here

X _____

Sign Here

X _____

Ref#: _____

Date/Time:

Signing Address:

Document Date	Notarization **Ack Jur Oth** Fee if any	Document Description	Signer Initials	
			1	2
		Deed of Trust / Mortgage		
		Deed - General - Quit Claim - Special Warranty		
		Borrower's Title Affidavit		
		Borrower's Closing Affidavit		
		E&O / Compliance Agreement		
		Occupancy Affidavit		
		Signature Name Affidavit		
		Power of Attorney - Limited / Durable		
		T-47 Residential Real Property Affidavit		
		Mineral Rights Acknowledgement and Agreement		

		Designation of Homestead / Non-Homestead		
		Notice of Penalties for Making False or Misleading Statements		
		Ownership Affidavit		
		Occupancy and Financial Status Affidavit		
		Obligation of Debts Affidavit		
		Release of Claims and Hold Harmless Agreement		
		Affidavit of Marital Status		
		Tax Indemnity		
		Compliance / Correction Agreement		

Notes:

Ack:Do you acknowledge this as your signature and your free act and deed, for the purposes stated herein?
Jurat: Do you solemnly (swear/affirm) that this statement is true, (so help you God / on your honor)?

Signer 1 Name and Address:		Signer 2 Name and Address:	
Identification Method: ☐ Personally Known ☐ Other ☐ Texas Driver's License ☐ Driver's License ☐ Passport		Identification Method: ☐ Personally Known ☐ Other ☐ Texas Driver's License ☐ Driver's License ☐ Passport	

Sign Here

X _____

Sign Here

X _____

Date/Time: _____   Ref#: _____

Signing Address: _____

Document Date	Notarization Ack Jur Oth Fee if any	Document Description	Signer Initials	
			1	2
		Deed of Trust / Mortgage		
		Deed – General – Quit Claim – Special Warranty		
		Borrower's Title Affidavit		
		Borrower's Closing Affidavit		
		E&O / Compliance Agreement		
		Occupancy Affidavit		
		Signature Name Affidavit		
		Power of Attorney – Limited / Durable		
		T-47 Residential Real Property Affidavit		
		Mineral Rights Acknowledgement and Agreement		

Designation of Homestead / Non-Homestead				
Notice of Penalties for Making False or Misleading Statements				
Ownership Affidavit				
Occupancy and Financial Status Affidavit				
Obligation of Debts Affidavit				
Release of Claims and Hold Harmless Agreement				
Affidavit of Marital Status				
Tax Indemnity				
Compliance / Correction Agreement				

Notes:

63 Ack: Do you acknowledge this as your signature and your free act and deed, for the purposes stated herein?
Jurat: Do you solemnly (swear/affirm) that this statement is true, (so help you God / on your honor)?

Signer 1 Name and Address:

Signer 2 Name and Address:

Identification Method: ☐ Personally Known ☐ Other
☐ Texas Driver's License ☐ Driver's License ☐ Passport

Identification Method: ☐ Personally Known ☐ Other
☐ Texas Driver's License ☐ Driver's License ☐ Passport

Sign Here

X _____

Sign Here

X _____

Date/Time:

Ref #:

Signing Address:

Document Date	Notarization Ack **Jur O**th Fee if any	Document Description	Signer Initials	
			1	2
		Deed of Trust / Mortgage		
		Deed - General - Quit Claim - Special Warranty		
		Borrower's Title Affidavit		
		Borrower's Closing Affidavit		
		E&O / Compliance Agreement		
		Occupancy Affidavit		
		Signature Name Affidavit		
		Power of Attorney - Limited / Durable		
		T-47 Residential Real Property Affidavit		
		Mineral Rights Acknowledgement and Agreement		

Designation of Homestead / Non-Homestead		
Notice of Penalties for Making False or Misleading Statements		
Ownership Affidavit		
Occupancy and Financial Status Affidavit		
Obligation of Debts Affidavit		
Release of Claims and Hold Harmless Agreement		
Affidavit of Marital Status		
Tax Indemnity		
Compliance / Correction Agreement		

Notes:

65 Ack: Do you acknowledge this as your signature and your free act and deed, for the purposes stated herein?
Jurat: Do you solemnly (swear/affirm) that this statement is true, (so help you God / on your honor)?

Signer 1 Name and Address:

Identification Method: ☐ Personally Known ☐ Other
☐ Texas Driver's License ☐ Driver's License ☐ Passport

Sign Here

X _____

Date/Time:

Signing Address:

Signer 2 Name and Address:

Identification Method: ☐ Personally Known ☐ Other
☐ Texas Driver's License ☐ Driver's License ☐ Passport

Sign Here

X _____   Ref # :

Document Date	Notarization Ack **J**ur **O**th Fee if any	Document Description	Signer Initials	
			1	2
		Deed of Trust / Mortgage		
		Deed - General - Quit Claim - Special Warranty		
		Borrower's Title Affidavit		
		Borrower's Closing Affidavit		
		E&O / Compliance Agreement		
		Occupancy Affidavit		
		Signature Name Affidavit		
		Power of Attorney - Limited / Durable		
		T-47 Residential Real Property Affidavit		
		Mineral Rights Acknowledgement and Agreement		

	Designation of Homestead / Non-Homestead
	Notice of Penalties for Making False or Misleading Statements
	Ownership Affidavit
	Occupancy and Financial Status Affidavit
	Obligation of Debts Affidavit
	Release of Claims and Hold Harmless Agreement
	Affidavit of Marital Status
	Tax Indemnity
	Compliance / Correction Agreement

Notes:

Ack: Do you acknowledge this as your signature and your free act and deed, for the purposes stated herein?
Jurat: Do you solemnly (swear/affirm) that this statement is true, (so help you God / on your honor)?

67

Signer 1 Name and Address:

Signer 2 Name and Address:

Identification Method: ☐ Personally Known ☐ Other
☐ Texas Driver's License ☐ Driver's License ☐ Passport

Identification Method: ☐ Personally Known ☐ Other
☐ Texas Driver's License ☐ Driver's License ☐ Passport

Sign Here

Sign Here

X _____

X _____

Date/Time: _____   Ref#: _____

Signing Address:

Document Date	Notarization Ack **J**ur **O**th Fee if any	Document Description	Signer Initials	
			1	2
		Deed of Trust / Mortgage		
		Deed – General – Quit Claim – Special Warranty		
		Borrower's Title Affidavit		
		Borrower's Closing Affidavit		
		E&O / Compliance Agreement		
		Occupancy Affidavit		
		Signature Name Affidavit		
		Power of Attorney – Limited / Durable		
		T-47 Residential Real Property Affidavit		
		Mineral Rights Acknowledgement and Agreement		

	Designation of Homestead / Non-Homestead
	Notice of Penalties for Making False or Misleading Statements
	Ownership Affidavit
	Occupancy and Financial Status Affidavit
	Obligation of Debts Affidavit
	Release of Claims and Hold Harmless Agreement
	Affidavit of Marital Status
	Tax Indemnity
	Compliance / Correction Agreement

Notes:

69 Ack: Do you acknowledge this as your signature and your free act and deed, for the purposes stated herein?
Jurat: Do you solemnly (swear/affirm) that this statement is true, (so help you God / on your honor)?

Signer 1 Name
and Address:

Signer 2 Name
and Address:

Identification Method: ☐ Personally Known ☐ Other
☐ Texas Driver's License ☐ Driver's License ☐ Passport

Identification Method: ☐ Personally Known ☐ Other
☐ Texas Driver's License ☐ Driver's License ☐ Passport

Sign Here

Sign Here

X _____

X _____

Date/Time:

Ref#:

Signing Address:

Document Date	Notarization Ack Jur Oth Fee if any	Document Description	Signer Initials	
			1	2
		Deed of Trust / Mortgage		
		Deed - General - Quit Claim - Special Warranty		
		Borrower's Title Affidavit		
		Borrower's Closing Affidavit		
		E&O / Compliance Agreement		
		Occupancy Affidavit		
		Signature Name Affidavit		
		Power of Attorney - Limited / Durable		
		T-47 Residential Real Property Affidavit		
		Mineral Rights Acknowledgement and Agreement		

		Designation of Homestead / Non-Homestead													
		Notice of Penalties for Making False or Misleading Statements													
		Ownership Affidavit													
		Occupancy and Financial Status Affidavit													
		Obligation of Debts Affidavit													
		Release of Claims and Hold Harmless Agreement													
		Affidavit of Marital Status													
		Tax Indemnity													
		Compliance / Correction Agreement													

Notes:

71 Ack:Do you acknowledge this as your signature and your free act and deed, for the purposes stated herein?
Jurat: Do you solemnly (swear/affirm) that this statement is true, (so help you God / on your honor)?

| Signer 1 Name and Address: | | Signer 2 Name and Address: | |

Identification Method: ☐ Personally Known ☐ Other ☐ Texas Driver's License ☐ Driver's License ☐ Passport

Identification Method: ☐ Personally Known ☐ Other ☐ Texas Driver's License ☐ Driver's License ☐ Passport

Sign Here

Sign Here

X _____

X _____ Ref #:

Date/Time:

Signing Address:

Document Date	Notarization Ack **J**ur **O**th Fee if any	Document Description	Signer Initials	
			1	2
		Deed of Trust / Mortgage		
		Deed - General - Quit Claim - Special Warranty		
		Borrower's Title Affidavit		
		Borrower's Closing Affidavit		
		E&O / Compliance Agreement		
		Occupancy Affidavit		
		Signature Name Affidavit		
		Power of Attorney - Limited / Durable		
		T-47 Residential Real Property Affidavit		
		Mineral Rights Acknowledgement and Agreement		

Designation of Homestead / Non-Homestead	Notice of Penalties for Making False or Misleading Statements	Ownership Affidavit	Occupancy and Financial Status Affidavit	Obligation of Debts Affidavit	Release of Claims and Hold Harmless Agreement	Affidavit of Marital Status	Tax Indemnity	Compliance / Correction Agreement						

Notes:

Ack: Do you acknowledge this as your signature and your free act and deed, for the purposes stated herein?
Jurat: Do you solemnly (swear/affirm) that this statement is true, (so help you God / on your honor)?

73

Signer 1 Name and Address:

Identification Method: ☐ Personally Known ☐ Other
☐ Texas Driver's License ☐ Driver's License ☐ Passport

Signer 2 Name and Address:

Identification Method: ☐ Personally Known ☐ Other
☐ Texas Driver's License ☐ Driver's License ☐ Passport

Sign Here

X _____

Sign Here

X _____

Date/Time: _____ Ref#: _____

Signing Address:

Document Date	Notarization Ack Jur Oth Fee if any	Document Description	Signer Initials 1	2
		Deed of Trust / Mortgage		
		Deed - General - Quit Claim - Special Warranty		
		Borrower's Title Affidavit		
		Borrower's Closing Affidavit		
		E&O / Compliance Agreement		
		Occupancy Affidavit		
		Signature Name Affidavit		
		Power of Attorney - Limited / Durable		
		T-47 Residential Real Property Affidavit		
		Mineral Rights Acknowledgement and Agreement		

	Designation of Homestead / Non-Homestead	Notice of Penalties for Making False or Misleading Statements	Ownership Affidavit	Occupancy and Financial Status Affidavit	Obligation of Debts Affidavit	Release of Claims and Hold Harmless Agreement	Affidavit of Marital Status	Tax Indemnity	Compliance / Correction Agreement								

Notes:

Ack:Do you acknowledge this as your signature and your free act and deed, for the purposes stated herein?
Jurat: Do you solemnly (swear/affirm) that this statement is true, (so help you God / on your honor)?

| Signer 1 Name and Address: | | Signer 2 Name and Address: | |

Signer 1 Name and Address:

Identification Method: ☐ Personally Known ☐ Other
☐ Texas Driver's License ☐ Driver's License ☐ Passport

Signer 2 Name and Address:

Identification Method: ☐ Personally Known ☐ Other
☐ Texas Driver's License ☐ Driver's License ☐ Passport

Sign Here

Sign Here

X _____

X _____

Date/Time:

Ref#:

Signing Address:

Document Date	Notarization Ack Jur Oth Fee if any	Document Description	Signer Initials	
			1	2
		Deed of Trust / Mortgage		
		Deed - General - Quit Claim - Special Warranty		
		Borrower's Title Affidavit		
		Borrower's Closing Affidavit		
		E&O / Compliance Agreement		
		Occupancy Affidavit		
		Signature Name Affidavit		
		Power of Attorney - Limited / Durable		
		T-47 Residential Real Property Affidavit		
		Mineral Rights Acknowledgement and Agreement		

	Designation of Homestead / Non-Homestead
	Notice of Penalties for Making False or Misleading Statements
	Ownership Affidavit
	Occupancy and Financial Status Affidavit
	Obligation of Debts Affidavit
	Release of Claims and Hold Harmless Agreement
	Affidavit of Marital Status
	Tax Indemnity
	Compliance / Correction Agreement

Notes:

77 Ack:Do you acknowledge this as your signature and your free act and deed, for the purposes stated herein?
Jurat: Do you solemnly (swear/affirm) that this statement is true, (so help you God / on your honor)?

Signer 1 Name and Address:

Signer 2 Name and Address:

Identification Method: ☐ Personally Known ☐ Other
☐ Texas Driver's License ☐ Driver's License ☐ Passport

Identification Method: ☐ Personally Known ☐ Other
☐ Texas Driver's License ☐ Driver's License ☐ Passport

Sign Here

Sign Here

X _____

X _____

Date/Time:

Ref#:

Signing Address:

Document Date	Notarization Ack **J**ur **O**th Fee if any	Document Description	Signer Initials 1	Signer Initials 2
		Deed of Trust / Mortgage		
		Deed - General - Quit Claim - Special Warranty		
		Borrower's Title Affidavit		
		Borrower's Closing Affidavit		
		E&O / Compliance Agreement		
		Occupancy Affidavit		
		Signature Name Affidavit		
		Power of Attorney - Limited / Durable		
		T-47 Residential Real Property Affidavit		
		Mineral Rights Acknowledgement and Agreement		

		Designation of Homestead / Non-Homestead											
		Notice of Penalties for Making False or Misleading Statements											
		Ownership Affidavit											
		Occupancy and Financial Status Affidavit											
		Obligation of Debts Affidavit											
		Release of Claims and Hold Harmless Agreement											
		Affidavit of Marital Status											
		Tax Indemnity											
		Compliance / Correction Agreement											

Notes:

79 Ack: Do you acknowledge this as your signature and your free act and deed, for the purposes stated herein?
Jurat: Do you solemnly (swear/affirm) that this statement is true, (so help you God / on your honor)?

Signer 1 Name and Address:

Signer 2 Name and Address:

Identification Method: ☐ Personally Known ☐ Other
☐ Texas Driver's License ☐ Driver's License ☐ Passport

Identification Method: ☐ Personally Known ☐ Other
☐ Texas Driver's License ☐ Driver's License ☐ Passport

Sign Here

Sign Here

X

X

Date/Time:

Ref#:

Signing Address:

Document Date	Notarization Ack Jur Oth Fee if any	Document Description	Signer Initials	
			1	2
		Deed of Trust / Mortgage		
		Deed - General - Quit Claim - Special Warranty		
		Borrower's Title Affidavit		
		Borrower's Closing Affidavit		
		E&O / Compliance Agreement		
		Occupancy Affidavit		
		Signature Name Affidavit		
		Power of Attorney - Limited / Durable		
		T-47 Residential Real Property Affidavit		
		Mineral Rights Acknowledgement and Agreement		

Designation of Homestead / Non-Homestead	
Notice of Penalties for Making False or Misleading Statements	
Ownership Affidavit	
Occupancy and Financial Status Affidavit	
Obligation of Debts Affidavit	
Release of Claims and Hold Harmless Agreement	
Affidavit of Marital Status	
Tax Indemnity	
Compliance / Correction Agreement	

Notes:

Ack: Do you acknowledge this as your signature and your free act and deed, for the purposes stated herein?
Jurat: Do you solemnly (swear/affirm) that this statement is true, (so help you God / on your honor)?

Signer 1 Name
and Address:

Signer 2 Name
and Address:

Identification Method: ☐ Personally Known   ☐ Other
☐ Texas Driver's License ☐ Driver's License ☐ Passport

Identification Method: ☐ Personally Known   ☐ Other
☐ Texas Driver's License ☐ Driver's License ☐ Passport

Sign Here

Sign Here

X

X

Date/Time:

Ref#:

Signing Address:

Document Date	Notarization **A**ck **J**ur **O**th Fee if any	Document Description	Signer Initials	
			1	2
		Deed of Trust / Mortgage		
		Deed - General - Quit Claim - Special Warranty		
		Borrower's Title Affidavit		
		Borrower's Closing Affidavit		
		E&O / Compliance Agreement		
		Occupancy Affidavit		
		Signature Name Affidavit		
		Power of Attorney - Limited / Durable		
		T-47 Residential Real Property Affidavit		
		Mineral Rights Acknowledgement and Agreement		

Designation of Homestead / Non-Homestead			
Notice of Penalties for Making False or Misleading Statements			
Ownership Affidavit			
Occupancy and Financial Status Affidavit			
Obligation of Debts Affidavit			
Release of Claims and Hold Harmless Agreement			
Affidavit of Marital Status			
Tax Indemnity			
Compliance / Correction Agreement			

Notes:

Ack: Do you acknowledge this as your signature and your free act and deed, for the purposes stated herein?
Jurat: Do you solemnly (swear/affirm) that this statement is true, (so help you God / on your honor)?

Signer 1 Name
and Address:

Signer 2 Name
and Address:

Identification Method: ☐ Personally Known ☐ Other
☐ Texas Driver's License ☐ Driver's License ☐ Passport

Identification Method: ☐ Personally Known ☐ Other
☐ Texas Driver's License ☐ Driver's License ☐ Passport

Sign Here

Sign Here

X _____

X _____

Date/Time: _____   Ref#: _____

Signing Address:

Document Date	Notarization Ack Jur Oth Fee if any	Document Description	Signer Initials	
			1	2
		Deed of Trust / Mortgage		
		Deed - General - Quit Claim - Special Warranty		
		Borrower's Title Affidavit		
		Borrower's Closing Affidavit		
		E&O / Compliance Agreement		
		Occupancy Affidavit		
		Signature Name Affidavit		
		Power of Attorney - Limited / Durable		
		T-47 Residential Real Property Affidavit		
		Mineral Rights Acknowledgement and Agreement		

	Designation of Homestead / Non-Homestead
	Notice of Penalties for Making False or Misleading Statements
	Ownership Affidavit
	Occupancy and Financial Status Affidavit
	Obligation of Debts Affidavit
	Release of Claims and Hold Harmless Agreement
	Affidavit of Marital Status
	Tax Indemnity
	Compliance / Correction Agreement

Notes:

Ack:Do you acknowledge this as your signature and your free act and deed, for the purposes stated herein?
Jurat: Do you solemnly (swear/affirm) that this statement is true, (so help you God / on your honor)?

| Signer 1 Name and Address: | | Signer 2 Name and Address: | |

Identification Method: □ Personally Known □ Other
□ Texas Driver's License □ Driver's License □ Passport

Identification Method: □ Personally Known □ Other
□ Texas Driver's License □ Driver's License □ Passport

Sign Here

Sign Here

X _____

X _____

Date/Time:

Ref#:

Signing Address:

Document Date	Notarization Ack Jur Oth Fee if any	Document Description	Signer Initials	
			1	2
		Deed of Trust / Mortgage		
		Deed - General - Quit Claim - Special Warranty		
		Borrower's Title Affidavit		
		Borrower's Closing Affidavit		
		E&O / Compliance Agreement		
		Occupancy Affidavit		
		Signature Name Affidavit		
		Power of Attorney - Limited / Durable		
		T-47 Residential Real Property Affidavit		
		Mineral Rights Acknowledgement and Agreement		

Document
Designation of Homestead / Non-Homestead
Notice of Penalties for Making False or Misleading Statements
Ownership Affidavit
Occupancy and Financial Status Affidavit
Obligation of Debts Affidavit
Release of Claims and Hold Harmless Agreement
Affidavit of Marital Status
Tax Indemnity
Compliance / Correction Agreement

Notes:

Ack:Do you acknowledge this as your signature and your free act and deed, for the purposes stated herein?
Jurat: Do you solemnly (swear/affirm) that this statement is true, (so help you God / on your honor)?

| Signer 1 Name and Address: | | Signer 2 Name and Address: | |

Identification Method: ☐ Personally Known ☐ Other
☐ Texas Driver's License ☐ Driver's License ☐ Passport

Identification Method: ☐ Personally Known ☐ Other
☐ Texas Driver's License ☐ Driver's License ☐ Passport

Sign Here

Sign Here

X _____ X _____

Date/Time: _____ Ref#: _____

Signing Address:

Document Date	Notarization Ack **J**ur **O**th Fee if any	Document Description	Signer Initials	
			1	2
		Deed of Trust / Mortgage		
		Deed - General - Quit Claim - Special Warranty		
		Borrower's Title Affidavit		
		Borrower's Closing Affidavit		
		E&O / Compliance Agreement		
		Occupancy Affidavit		
		Signature Name Affidavit		
		Power of Attorney - Limited / Durable		
		T-47 Residential Real Property Affidavit		
		Mineral Rights Acknowledgement and Agreement		

Designation of Homestead / Non-Homestead	
Notice of Penalties for Making False or Misleading Statements	
Ownership Affidavit	
Occupancy and Financial Status Affidavit	
Obligation of Debts Affidavit	
Release of Claims and Hold Harmless Agreement	
Affidavit of Marital Status	
Tax Indemnity	
Compliance / Correction Agreement	

Notes:

Ack:Do you acknowledge this as your signature and your free act and deed, for the purposes stated herein?
Jurat: Do you solemnly (swear/affirm) that this statement is true, (so help you God / on your honor)?

Signer 1 Name
and Address:

Signer 2 Name
and Address:

Identification Method:☐ Personally Known ☐ Other
☐ Texas Driver's License ☐ Driver's License ☐ Passport

Identification Method:☐ Personally Known ☐ Other
☐ Texas Driver's License ☐ Driver's License ☐ Passport

Sign Here

Sign Here

X _____

X _____

Date/Time:

Ref#:

Signing Address:

Document Date	Notarization Ack **J**ur **O**th Fee if any	Document Description	Signer Initials	
			1	2
		Deed of Trust / Mortgage		
		Deed - General - Quit Claim - Special Warranty		
		Borrower's Title Affidavit		
		Borrower's Closing Affidavit		
		E&O / Compliance Agreement		
		Occupancy Affidavit		
		Signature Name Affidavit		
		Power of Attorney - Limited / Durable		
		T-47 Residential Real Property Affidavit		
		Mineral Rights Acknowledgement and Agreement		

		Designation of Homestead / Non-Homestead
		Notice of Penalties for Making False or Misleading Statements
		Ownership Affidavit
		Occupancy and Financial Status Affidavit
		Obligation of Debts Affidavit
		Release of Claims and Hold Harmless Agreement
		Affidavit of Marital Status
		Tax Indemnity
		Compliance / Correction Agreement

Notes:

91   Ack:Do you acknowledge this as your signature and your free act and deed, for the purposes stated herein?
Jurat: Do you solemnly (swear/affirm) that this statement is true, (so help you God / on your honor)?

Signer 1 Name and Address:

Identification Method: ☐ Personally Known ☐ Other
☐ Texas Driver's License ☐ Passport

Signer 2 Name and Address:

Identification Method: ☐ Personally Known ☐ Other
☐ Texas Driver's License ☐ Passport

Sign Here

X _____

Sign Here

X _____

Date/Time: **Ref #:**

Signing Address:

Document Date	Notarization Ack **Jur** **Oth** Fee if any	Document Description	Signer Initials 1	2
		Deed of Trust / Mortgage		
		Deed - General - Quit Claim - Special Warranty		
		Borrower's Title Affidavit		
		Borrower's Closing Affidavit		
		E&O / Compliance Agreement		
		Occupancy Affidavit		
		Signature Name Affidavit		
		Power of Attorney - Limited / Durable		
		T-47 Residential Real Property Affidavit		
		Mineral Rights Acknowledgement and Agreement		

Designation of Homestead / Non-Homestead	Notice of Penalties for Making False or Misleading Statements	Ownership Affidavit	Occupancy and Financial Status Affidavit	Obligation of Debts Affidavit	Release of Claims and Hold Harmless Agreement	Affidavit of Marital Status	Tax Indemnity	Compliance / Correction Agreement	

Notes:

Ack: Do you acknowledge this as your signature and your free act and deed, for the purposes stated herein?

Jurat: Do you solemnly (swear/affirm) that this statement is true, (so help you God / on your honor)?

Signer 1 Name
and Address:

Signer 2 Name
and Address:

Identification Method: ☐ Personally Known ☐ Other
☐ Texas Driver's License ☐ Driver's License ☐ Passport

Identification Method: ☐ Personally Known ☐ Other
☐ Texas Driver's License ☐ Driver's License ☐ Passport

Sign Here

Sign Here

X _____

X _____

Date/Time:

Ref#:

Signing Address:

Document Date	Notarization Ack Jur Oth Fee if any	Document Description	Signer Initials	
			1	2
		Deed of Trust / Mortgage		
		Deed - General - Quit Claim - Special Warranty		
		Borrower's Title Affidavit		
		Borrower's Closing Affidavit		
		E&O / Compliance Agreement		
		Occupancy Affidavit		
		Signature Name Affidavit		
		Power of Attorney - Limited / Durable		
		T-47 Residential Real Property Affidavit		
		Mineral Rights Acknowledgement and Agreement		

		Designation of Homestead / Non-Homestead
		Notice of Penalties for Making False or Misleading Statements
		Ownership Affidavit
		Occupancy and Financial Status Affidavit
		Obligation of Debts Affidavit
		Release of Claims and Hold Harmless Agreement
		Affidavit of Marital Status
		Tax Indemnity
		Compliance / Correction Agreement

Notes:

Ack:Do you acknowledge this as your signature and your free act and deed, for the purposes stated herein?
Jurat: Do you solemnly (swear/affirm) that this statement is true, (so help you God / on your honor)?

Signer 1 Name and Address:		Signer 2 Name and Address:	
Identification Method: ☐ Personally Known ☐ Other ☐ Texas Driver's License ☐ Driver's License ☐ Passport		Identification Method: ☐ Personally Known ☐ Other ☐ Texas Driver's License ☐ Driver's License ☐ Passport	

Sign Here

X _____

Sign Here

X _____

Ref#: _____

Date/Time:

Signing Address:

Document Date	Notarization Ack Jur Oth Fee if any	Document Description	Signer Initials	
			1	2
		Deed of Trust / Mortgage		
		Deed - General - Quit Claim - Special Warranty		
		Borrower's Title Affidavit		
		Borrower's Closing Affidavit		
		E&O / Compliance Agreement		
		Occupancy Affidavit		
		Signature Name Affidavit		
		Power of Attorney - Limited / Durable		
		T-47 Residential Real Property Affidavit		
		Mineral Rights Acknowledgement and Agreement		

| Designation of Homestead / Non-Homestead |
| Notice of Penalties for Making False or Misleading Statements |
| Ownership Affidavit |
| Occupancy and Financial Status Affidavit |
| Obligation of Debts Affidavit |
| Release of Claims and Hold Harmless Agreement |
| Affidavit of Marital Status |
| Tax Indemnity |
| Compliance / Correction Agreement |

Notes:

Ack: Do you acknowledge this as your signature and your free act and deed, for the purposes stated herein?
Jurat: Do you solemnly (swear/affirm) that this statement is true, (so help you God / on your honor)?

Signer 1 Name and Address:

Signer 2 Name and Address:

Identification Method: ☐ Personally Known ☐ Other
☐ Texas Driver's License ☐ Driver's License ☐ Passport

Identification Method: ☐ Personally Known ☐ Other
☐ Texas Driver's License ☐ Driver's License ☐ Passport

Sign Here

X _____

Sign Here

X _____

Date/Time: _____ **Ref#:** _____

Signing Address:

Document Date	Notarization Ack Jur Oth Fee if any	Document Description	Signer Initials	
			1	2
		Deed of Trust / Mortgage		
		Deed - General - Quit Claim - Special Warranty		
		Borrower's Title Affidavit		
		Borrower's Closing Affidavit		
		E&O / Compliance Agreement		
		Occupancy Affidavit		
		Signature Name Affidavit		
		Power of Attorney - Limited / Durable		
		T-47 Residential Real Property Affidavit		
		Mineral Rights Acknowledgement and Agreement		

		Designation of Homestead / Non-Homestead
		Notice of Penalties for Making False or Misleading Statements
		Ownership Affidavit
		Occupancy and Financial Status Affidavit
		Obligation of Debts Affidavit
		Release of Claims and Hold Harmless Agreement
		Affidavit of Marital Status
		Tax Indemnity
		Compliance / Correction Agreement

Notes:

99   Ack: Do you acknowledge this as your signature and your free act and deed, for the purposes stated herein?
Jurat: Do you solemnly (swear/affirm) that this statement is true, (so help you God / on your honor)?

Signer 1 Name
and Address:

Signer 2 Name
and Address:

Identification Method:☐ Personally Known   ☐ Other
☐ Texas Driver's License ☐ Driver's License ☐ Passport

Identification Method:☐ Personally Known   ☐ Other
☐ Texas Driver's License ☐ Driver's License ☐ Passport

Sign Here

Sign Here

X _____

X _____

Date/Time:

Ref#:

Signing Address:

Document Date	Notarization Ack **J**ur **O**th Fee if any	Document Description	Signer Initials	
			1	2
		Deed of Trust / Mortgage		
		Deed – General – Quit Claim – Special Warranty		
		Borrower's Title Affidavit		
		Borrower's Closing Affidavit		
		E&O / Compliance Agreement		
		Occupancy Affidavit		
		Signature Name Affidavit		
		Power of Attorney – Limited / Durable		
		T-47 Residential Real Property Affidavit		
		Mineral Rights Acknowledgement and Agreement		

		Designation of Homestead / Non-Homestead		
		Notice of Penalties for Making False or Misleading Statements		
		Ownership Affidavit		
		Occupancy and Financial Status Affidavit		
		Obligation of Debts Affidavit		
		Release of Claims and Hold Harmless Agreement		
		Affidavit of Marital Status		
		Tax Indemnity		
		Compliance / Correction Agreement		

Notes:

101 Ack:Do you acknowledge this as your signature and your free act and deed, for the purposes stated herein?
Jurat: Do you solemnly (swear/affirm) that this statement is true, (so help you God / on your honor)?

Signer 1 Name and Address:

Signer 2 Name and Address:

Identification Method: ☐ Personally Known ☐ Other
☐ Texas Driver's License ☐ Driver's License ☐ Passport

Identification Method: ☐ Personally Known ☐ Other
☐ Texas Driver's License ☐ Driver's License ☐ Passport

Sign Here

Sign Here

X _____

X _____

Date/Time: _____   Ref#: _____

Signing Address: _____

Document Date	Notarization Ack **J**ur **O**th Fee if any	Document Description	Signer Initials	
			1	2
		Deed of Trust / Mortgage		
		Deed - General - Quit Claim - Special Warranty		
		Borrower's Title Affidavit		
		Borrower's Closing Affidavit		
		E&O / Compliance Agreement		
		Occupancy Affidavit		
		Signature Name Affidavit		
		Power of Attorney - Limited / Durable		
		T-47 Residential Real Property Affidavit		
		Mineral Rights Acknowledgement and Agreement		

Designation of Homestead / Non-Homestead	Notice of Penalties for Making False or Misleading Statements	Ownership Affidavit	Occupancy and Financial Status Affidavit	Obligation of Debts Affidavit	Release of Claims and Hold Harmless Agreement	Affidavit of Marital Status	Tax Indemnity	Compliance / Correction Agreement					

Notes:

103 Ack:Do you acknowledge this as your signature and your free act and deed, for the purposes stated herein?
Jurat: Do you solemnly (swear/affirm) that this statement is true, (so help you God / on your honor)?

Signer 1 Name and Address:		Signer 2 Name and Address:

Identification Method: ☐ Personally Known ☐ Other
☐ Texas Driver's License ☐ Driver's License ☐ Passport

Identification Method: ☐ Personally Known ☐ Other
☐ Texas Driver's License ☐ Driver's License ☐ Passport

Sign Here

X _____

Date/Time:

X _____

Ref#:

Signing Address:

Document Date	Notarization **A**ck **J**ur **O**th Fee if any	Document Description	Signer Initials	
			1	2
		Deed of Trust / Mortgage		
		Deed - General - Quit Claim - Special Warranty		
		Borrower's Title Affidavit		
		Borrower's Closing Affidavit		
		E&O / Compliance Agreement		
		Occupancy Affidavit		
		Signature Name Affidavit		
		Power of Attorney - Limited / Durable		
		T-47 Residential Real Property Affidavit		
		Mineral Rights Acknowledgement and Agreement		

		Designation of Homestead / Non-Homestead	Notice of Penalties for Making False or Misleading Statements	Ownership Affidavit	Occupancy and Financial Status Affidavit	Obligation of Debts Affidavit	Release of Claims and Hold Harmless Agreement	Affidavit of Marital Status	Tax Indemnity	Compliance / Correction Agreement									

Notes:

Ack: Do you acknowledge this as your signature and your free act and deed, for the purposes stated herein?
Jurat: Do you solemnly (swear/affirm) that this statement is true, (so help you God / on your honor)?

| Signer 1 Name and Address: | | | | Signer 2 Name and Address: | | |

Identification Method: ☐ Personally Known ☐ Other
☐ Texas Driver's License ☐ Driver's License ☐ Passport

Identification Method: ☐ Personally Known ☐ Other
☐ Texas Driver's License ☐ Driver's License ☐ Passport

Sign Here

X _____

Sign Here

X _____

Date/Time: _____   Ref#: _____

Signing Address:

Document Date	Notarization Ack Jur Oth Fee if any	Document Description	Signer Initials	
			1	2
		Deed of Trust / Mortgage		
		Deed – General – Quit Claim – Special Warranty		
		Borrower's Title Affidavit		
		Borrower's Closing Affidavit		
		E&O / Compliance Agreement		
		Occupancy Affidavit		
		Signature Name Affidavit		
		Power of Attorney – Limited / Durable		
		T-47 Residential Real Property Affidavit		
		Mineral Rights Acknowledgement and Agreement		

Designation of Homestead / Non-Homestead			
Notice of Penalties for Making False or Misleading Statements			
Ownership Affidavit			
Occupancy and Financial Status Affidavit			
Obligation of Debts Affidavit			
Release of Claims and Hold Harmless Agreement			
Affidavit of Marital Status			
Tax Indemnity			
Compliance / Correction Agreement			

Notes:

Ack: Do you acknowledge this as your signature and your free act and deed, for the purposes stated herein?

Jurat: Do you solemnly (swear/affirm) that this statement is true, (so help you God / on your honor)?

107

Signer 1 Name and Address:		Signer 2 Name and Address:	
Identification Method: ☐ Personally Known ☐ Other ☐ Texas Driver's License ☐ Driver's License ☐ Passport		Identification Method: ☐ Personally Known ☐ Other ☐ Texas Driver's License ☐ Driver's License ☐ Passport	

Sign Here

X _____

Sign Here

X _____

Date/Time: _____   **Ref #:** _____

Signing Address: _____

Document Date	Notarization **Ack Jur Oth** Fee if any	Document Description	Signer Initials	
			1	2
		Deed of Trust / Mortgage		
		Deed - General - Quit Claim - Special Warranty		
		Borrower's Title Affidavit		
		Borrower's Closing Affidavit		
		E&O / Compliance Agreement		
		Occupancy Affidavit		
		Signature Name Affidavit		
		Power of Attorney - Limited / Durable		
		T-47 Residential Real Property Affidavit		
		Mineral Rights Acknowledgement and Agreement		

	Designation of Homestead / Non-Homestead
	Notice of Penalties for Making False or Misleading Statements
	Ownership Affidavit
	Occupancy and Financial Status Affidavit
	Obligation of Debts Affidavit
	Release of Claims and Hold Harmless Agreement
	Affidavit of Marital Status
	Tax Indemnity
	Compliance / Correction Agreement

Notes:

Ack: Do you acknowledge this as your signature and your free act and deed, for the purposes stated herein?
Jurat: Do you solemnly (swear/affirm) that this statement is true, (so help you God / on your honor)?

| Signer 1 Name and Address: | | Signer 2 Name and Address: | |

Signer 1 Name and Address:

Signer 2 Name and Address:

Identification Method: ☐ Personally Known ☐ Other
☐ Texas Driver's License ☐ Driver's License ☐ Passport

Identification Method: ☐ Personally Known ☐ Other
☐ Texas Driver's License ☐ Driver's License ☐ Passport

Sign Here

Sign Here

X _____

X _____

Date/Time: _____   **Ref#:** _____

Signing Address: _____

Document Date	Notarization Ack **J**ur **O**th Fee if any	Document Description	Signer Initials	
			1	2
		Deed of Trust / Mortgage		
		Deed - General - Quit Claim - Special Warranty		
		Borrower's Title Affidavit		
		Borrower's Closing Affidavit		
		E&O / Compliance Agreement		
		Occupancy Affidavit		
		Signature Name Affidavit		
		Power of Attorney - Limited / Durable		
		T-47 Residential Real Property Affidavit		
		Mineral Rights Acknowledgement and Agreement		

		Designation of Homestead / Non-Homestead																		
		Notice of Penalties for Making False or Misleading Statements																		
		Ownership Affidavit																		
		Occupancy and Financial Status Affidavit																		
		Obligation of Debts Affidavit																		
		Release of Claims and Hold Harmless Agreement																		
		Affidavit of Marital Status																		
		Tax Indemnity																		
		Compliance / Correction Agreement																		

Notes:

111 Ack:Do you acknowledge this as your signature and your free act and deed, for the purposes stated herein?
Jurat: Do you solemnly (swear/affirm) that this statement is true, (so help you God / on your honor)?

Signer 1 Name and Address:

Signer 2 Name and Address:

Identification Method:☐ Personally Known ☐ Other
☐ Texas Driver's License ☐ Driver's License ☐ Passport

Identification Method:☐ Personally Known ☐ Other
☐ Texas Driver's License ☐ Driver's License ☐ Passport

Sign Here

Sign Here

X _____

X _____

Date/Time:

Ref#:

Signing Address:

Document Date	Notarization Ack Jur Oth Fee if any	Document Description	Signer Initials 1	2
		Deed of Trust / Mortgage		
		Deed - General - Quit Claim - Special Warranty		
		Borrower's Title Affidavit		
		Borrower's Closing Affidavit		
		E&O / Compliance Agreement		
		Occupancy Affidavit		
		Signature Name Affidavit		
		Power of Attorney - Limited / Durable		
		T-47 Residential Real Property Affidavit		
		Mineral Rights Acknowledgement and Agreement		

Designation of Homestead / Non-Homestead																					
Notice of Penalties for Making False or Misleading Statements																					
Ownership Affidavit																					
Occupancy and Financial Status Affidavit																					
Obligation of Debts Affidavit																					
Release of Claims and Hold Harmless Agreement																					
Affidavit of Marital Status																					
Tax Indemnity																					
Compliance / Correction Agreement																					

Notes:

113 Ack: Do you acknowledge this as your signature and your free act and deed, for the purposes stated herein?
Jurat: Do you solemnly (swear/affirm) that this statement is true, (so help you God / on your honor)?

Signer 1 Name and Address:

Signer 2 Name and Address:

Identification Method: ☐ Personally Known ☐ Other
☐ Texas Driver's License ☐ Driver's License ☐ Passport

Identification Method: ☐ Personally Known ☐ Other
☐ Texas Driver's License ☐ Driver's License ☐ Passport

Sign Here

Sign Here

X _____

X _____

Date/Time: Ref #:

Signing Address:

Document Date	Notarization Ack **Jur** **O**th Fee if any	Document Description	Signer Initials	
			1	2
		Deed of Trust / Mortgage		
		Deed - General - Quit Claim - Special Warranty		
		Borrower's Title Affidavit		
		Borrower's Closing Affidavit		
		E&O / Compliance Agreement		
		Occupancy Affidavit		
		Signature Name Affidavit		
		Power of Attorney - Limited / Durable		
		T-47 Residential Real Property Affidavit		
		Mineral Rights Acknowledgement and Agreement		

Designation of Homestead / Non-Homestead	
Notice of Penalties for Making False or Misleading Statements	
Ownership Affidavit	
Occupancy and Financial Status Affidavit	
Obligation of Debts Affidavit	
Release of Claims and Hold Harmless Agreement	
Affidavit of Marital Status	
Tax Indemnity	
Compliance / Correction Agreement	

Notes:

115 Ack: Do you acknowledge this as your signature and your free act and deed, for the purposes stated herein?
Jurat: Do you solemnly (swear/affirm) that this statement is true, (so help you God / on your honor)?

Signer 1 Name and Address:		Signer 2 Name and Address:	

Identification Method:☐ Personally Known ☐ Other ☐ Texas Driver's License ☐ Driver's License ☐ Passport	Identification Method:☐ Personally Known ☐ Other ☐ Texas Driver's License ☐ Driver's License ☐ Passport

Sign Here

X _____   X _____

Date/Time: _____   Ref#: _____

Signing Address:

Document Date	Notarization Ack Jur Oth Fee if any	Document Description	Signer Initials	
			1	2
		Deed of Trust / Mortgage		
		Deed - General - Quit Claim - Special Warranty		
		Borrower's Title Affidavit		
		Borrower's Closing Affidavit		
		E&O / Compliance Agreement		
		Occupancy Affidavit		
		Signature Name Affidavit		
		Power of Attorney - Limited / Durable		
		T-47 Residential Real Property Affidavit		
		Mineral Rights Acknowledgement and Agreement		

	Designation of Homestead / Non-Homestead
	Notice of Penalties for Making False or Misleading Statements
	Ownership Affidavit
	Occupancy and Financial Status Affidavit
	Obligation of Debts Affidavit
	Release of Claims and Hold Harmless Agreement
	Affidavit of Marital Status
	Tax Indemnity
	Compliance / Correction Agreement

Notes:

117 Ack:Do you acknowledge this as your signature and your free act and deed, for the purposes stated herein?
Jurat: Do you solemnly (swear/affirm) that this statement is true, (so help you God / on your honor)?

Signer 1 Name
and Address:

Signer 2 Name
and Address:

Identification Method:☐ Personally Known ☐ Other
☐ Texas Driver's License ☐ Driver's License ☐ Passport

Identification Method:☐ Personally Known ☐ Other
☐ Texas Driver's License ☐ Driver's License ☐ Passport

Sign Here

Sign Here

X _____

X _____

Date/Time:

Ref#:

Signing Address:

Document Date	Notarization Ack **J**ur **O**th Fee if any	Document Description	Signer Initials	
			1	2
		Deed of Trust / Mortgage		
		Deed – General – Quit Claim – Special Warranty		
		Borrower's Title Affidavit		
		Borrower's Closing Affidavit		
		E&O / Compliance Agreement		
		Occupancy Affidavit		
		Signature Name Affidavit		
		Power of Attorney – Limited / Durable		
		T-47 Residential Real Property Affidavit		
		Mineral Rights Acknowledgement and Agreement		

Document		
Designation of Homestead / Non-Homestead		
Notice of Penalties for Making False or Misleading Statements		
Ownership Affidavit		
Occupancy and Financial Status Affidavit		
Obligation of Debts Affidavit		
Release of Claims and Hold Harmless Agreement		
Affidavit of Marital Status		
Tax Indemnity		
Compliance / Correction Agreement		

Notes:

Ack:Do you acknowledge this as your signature and your free act and deed, for the purposes stated herein?
Jurat: Do you solemnly (swear/affirm) that this statement is true, (so help you God / on your honor)?

119

Signer 1 Name and Address:		Signer 2 Name and Address:	

Identification Method: ☐ Personally Known ☐ Other
☐ Texas Driver's License ☐ Driver's License ☐ Passport

Identification Method: ☐ Personally Known ☐ Other
☐ Texas Driver's License ☐ Driver's License ☐ Passport

Sign Here

Sign Here

X _____

X _____

Date/Time:

Ref#:

Signing Address:

Document Date	Notarization **Ack Jur Oth** Fee if any	Document Description	Signer Initials	
			1	2
		Deed of Trust / Mortgage		
		Deed - General - Quit Claim - Special Warranty		
		Borrower's Title Affidavit		
		Borrower's Closing Affidavit		
		E&O / Compliance Agreement		
		Occupancy Affidavit		
		Signature Name Affidavit		
		Power of Attorney - Limited / Durable		
		T-47 Residential Real Property Affidavit		
		Mineral Rights Acknowledgement and Agreement		

Document														
Designation of Homestead / Non-Homestead														
Notice of Penalties for Making False or Misleading Statements														
Ownership Affidavit														
Occupancy and Financial Status Affidavit														
Obligation of Debts Affidavit														
Release of Claims and Hold Harmless Agreement														
Affidavit of Marital Status														
Tax Indemnity														
Compliance / Correction Agreement														

Notes:

121 Ack: Do you acknowledge this as your signature and your free act and deed, for the purposes stated herein?
Jurat: Do you solemnly (swear/affirm) that this statement is true, (so help you God / on your honor)?

| Signer 1 Name and Address: | | Signer 2 Name and Address: | |

Identification Method: ☐ Personally Known ☐ Other
☐ Texas Driver's License ☐ Driver's License ☐ Passport

Identification Method: ☐ Personally Known ☐ Other
☐ Texas Driver's License ☐ Driver's License ☐ Passport

Sign Here

Sign Here

X _____

X _____

Date/Time: _____   Ref #: _____

Signing Address:

Document Date	Notarization Ack **Jur** Oth Fee if any	Document Description	Signer Initials	
			1	2
		Deed of Trust / Mortgage		
		Deed - General - Quit Claim - Special Warranty		
		Borrower's Title Affidavit		
		Borrower's Closing Affidavit		
		E&O / Compliance Agreement		
		Occupancy Affidavit		
		Signature Name Affidavit		
		Power of Attorney - Limited / Durable		
		T-47 Residential Real Property Affidavit		
		Mineral Rights Acknowledgement and Agreement		

		Designation of Homestead / Non-Homestead		
		Notice of Penalties for Making False or Misleading Statements		
		Ownership Affidavit		
		Occupancy and Financial Status Affidavit		
		Obligation of Debts Affidavit		
		Release of Claims and Hold Harmless Agreement		
		Affidavit of Marital Status		
		Tax Indemnity		
		Compliance / Correction Agreement		

Notes:

123 Ack:Do you acknowledge this as your signature and your free act and deed, for the purposes stated herein?
Jurat: Do you solemnly (swear/affirm) that this statement is true, (so help you God / on your honor)?

Signer 1 Name and Address:

Identification Method: ☐ Personally Known ☐ Other
☐ Texas Driver's License ☐ Driver's License ☐ Passport

Sign Here

X _____

Date/Time:

Signing Address:

Signer 2 Name and Address:

Identification Method: ☐ Personally Known ☐ Other
☐ Texas Driver's License ☐ Driver's License ☐ Passport

Sign Here

X _____

Ref #:

Document Date	Notarization Ack **J**ur **O**th Fee if any	Document Description	Signer Initials	
			1	2
		Deed of Trust / Mortgage		
		Deed - General - Quit Claim - Special Warranty		
		Borrower's Title Affidavit		
		Borrower's Closing Affidavit		
		E&O / Compliance Agreement		
		Occupancy Affidavit		
		Signature Name Affidavit		
		Power of Attorney - Limited / Durable		
		T-47 Residential Real Property Affidavit		
		Mineral Rights Acknowledgement and Agreement		

Designation of Homestead / Non-Homestead		
Notice of Penalties for Making False or Misleading Statements		
Ownership Affidavit		
Occupancy and Financial Status Affidavit		
Obligation of Debts Affidavit		
Release of Claims and Hold Harmless Agreement		
Affidavit of Marital Status		
Tax Indemnity		
Compliance / Correction Agreement		

Notes:

Ack: Do you acknowledge this as your signature and your free act and deed, for the purposes stated herein?

Jurat: Do you solemnly (swear/affirm) that this statement is true, (so help you God / on your honor)?

| Signer 1 Name and Address: | | Signer 2 Name and Address: | |

Signer 1 Name and Address:

Identification Method: ☐ Personally Known ☐ Other
☐ Texas Driver's License ☐ Driver's License ☐ Passport

Signer 2 Name and Address:

Identification Method: ☐ Personally Known ☐ Other
☐ Texas Driver's License ☐ Driver's License ☐ Passport

Sign Here

Sign Here

X _____

X _____

Date/Time: Ref #:

Signing Address:

Document Date	Notarization Ack **J**ur **O**th Fee if any	Document Description	Signer Initials	
			1	2
		Deed of Trust / Mortgage		
		Deed - General - Quit Claim - Special Warranty		
		Borrower's Title Affidavit		
		Borrower's Closing Affidavit		
		E&O / Compliance Agreement		
		Occupancy Affidavit		
		Signature Name Affidavit		
		Power of Attorney - Limited / Durable		
		T-47 Residential Real Property Affidavit		
		Mineral Rights Acknowledgement and Agreement		

Document		
Designation of Homestead / Non-Homestead		
Notice of Penalties for Making False or Misleading Statements		
Ownership Affidavit		
Occupancy and Financial Status Affidavit		
Obligation of Debts Affidavit		
Release of Claims and Hold Harmless Agreement		
Affidavit of Marital Status		
Tax Indemnity		
Compliance / Correction Agreement		

Notes:

127 Ack: Do you acknowledge this as your signature and your free act and deed, for the purposes stated herein?
Jurat: Do you solemnly (swear/affirm) that this statement is true, (so help you God / on your honor)?

| Signer 1 Name and Address: | | Signer 2 Name and Address: | |

Signer 1
Identification Method: ☐ Personally Known ☐ Other
☐ Texas Driver's License ☐ Driver's License ☐ Passport

Signer 2
Identification Method: ☐ Personally Known ☐ Other
☐ Texas Driver's License ☐ Driver's License ☐ Passport

Sign Here

X _____ X _____

Ref # : _____

Date/Time: _____

Signing Address:

Document Date	Notarization Ack **J**ur **O**th Fee if any	Document Description	Signer Initials	
			1	2
		Deed of Trust / Mortgage		
		Deed - General - Quit Claim - Special Warranty		
		Borrower's Title Affidavit		
		Borrower's Closing Affidavit		
		E&O / Compliance Agreement		
		Occupancy Affidavit		
		Signature Name Affidavit		
		Power of Attorney - Limited / Durable		
		T-47 Residential Real Property Affidavit		
		Mineral Rights Acknowledgement and Agreement		

	Designation of Homestead / Non-Homestead
	Notice of Penalties for Making False or Misleading Statements
	Ownership Affidavit
	Occupancy and Financial Status Affidavit
	Obligation of Debts Affidavit
	Release of Claims and Hold Harmless Agreement
	Affidavit of Marital Status
	Tax Indemnity
	Compliance / Correction Agreement

Notes:

129 Ack: Do you acknowledge this as your signature and your free act and deed, for the purposes stated herein?
Jurat: Do you solemnly (swear/affirm) that this statement is true, (so help you God / on your honor)?

| Signer 1 Name and Address: | | Signer 2 Name and Address: | |

Identification Method: ☐ Personally Known ☐ Other
☐ Texas Driver's License ☐ Driver's License ☐ Passport

Identification Method: ☐ Personally Known ☐ Other
☐ Texas Driver's License ☐ Driver's License ☐ Passport

Sign Here

Sign Here

X _____

X _____

Ref#:

Date/Time:

Signing Address:

Document Date	Notarization Ack **Jur** **O**th Fee if any	Document Description	Signer Initials	
			1	2
		Deed of Trust / Mortgage		
		Deed - General - Quit Claim - Special Warranty		
		Borrower's Title Affidavit		
		Borrower's Closing Affidavit		
		E&O / Compliance Agreement		
		Occupancy Affidavit		
		Signature Name Affidavit		
		Power of Attorney - Limited / Durable		
		T-47 Residential Real Property Affidavit		
		Mineral Rights Acknowledgement and Agreement		

Designation of Homestead / Non-Homestead	
Notice of Penalties for Making False or Misleading Statements	
Ownership Affidavit	
Occupancy and Financial Status Affidavit	
Obligation of Debts Affidavit	
Release of Claims and Hold Harmless Agreement	
Affidavit of Marital Status	
Tax Indemnity	
Compliance / Correction Agreement	

Notes:

131 Ack:Do you acknowledge this as your signature and your free act and deed, for the purposes stated herein?
Jurat: Do you solemnly (swear/affirm) that this statement is true, (so help you God / on your honor)?

Signer 1 Name and Address:			Signer 2 Name and Address:		

Identification Method: ☐ Personally Known ☐ Other
☐ Texas Driver's License ☐ Driver's License ☐ Passport

Identification Method: ☐ Personally Known ☐ Other
☐ Texas Driver's License ☐ Driver's License ☐ Passport

Sign Here

Sign Here

X _____

X _____   Ref#: _____

Date/Time:

Signing Address:

Document Date	Notarization Ack Jur Oth Fee if any	Document Description	Signer Initials	
			1	2
		Deed of Trust / Mortgage		
		Deed - General - Quit Claim - Special Warranty		
		Borrower's Title Affidavit		
		Borrower's Closing Affidavit		
		E&O / Compliance Agreement		
		Occupancy Affidavit		
		Signature Name Affidavit		
		Power of Attorney - Limited / Durable		
		T-47 Residential Real Property Affidavit		
		Mineral Rights Acknowledgement and Agreement		

	Designation of Homestead / Non-Homestead
	Notice of Penalties for Making False or Misleading Statements
	Ownership Affidavit
	Occupancy and Financial Status Affidavit
	Obligation of Debts Affidavit
	Release of Claims and Hold Harmless Agreement
	Affidavit of Marital Status
	Tax Indemnity
	Compliance / Correction Agreement

Notes:

133 Ack: Do you acknowledge this as your signature and your free act and deed, for the purposes stated herein?
Jurat: Do you solemnly (swear/affirm) that this statement is true, (so help you God / on your honor)?

Signer 1 Name and Address:

Identification Method: ☐ Personally Known ☐ Other
☐ Texas Driver's License ☐ Driver's License ☐ Passport

Sign Here

X _____

Date/Time:

Signer 2 Name and Address:

Identification Method: ☐ Personally Known ☐ Other
☐ Texas Driver's License ☐ Driver's License ☐ Passport

Sign Here

X _____

Ref #:

Signing Address:

Document Date	Notarization Ack Jur Oth Fee if any	Document Description	Signer Initials 1	2
		Deed of Trust / Mortgage		
		Deed - General - Quit Claim - Special Warranty		
		Borrower's Title Affidavit		
		Borrower's Closing Affidavit		
		E&O / Compliance Agreement		
		Occupancy Affidavit		
		Signature Name Affidavit		
		Power of Attorney - Limited / Durable		
		T-47 Residential Real Property Affidavit		
		Mineral Rights Acknowledgement and Agreement		

		Designation of Homestead / Non-Homestead
		Notice of Penalties for Making False or Misleading Statements
		Ownership Affidavit
		Occupancy and Financial Status Affidavit
		Obligation of Debts Affidavit
		Release of Claims and Hold Harmless Agreement
		Affidavit of Marital Status
		Tax Indemnity
		Compliance / Correction Agreement

Notes:

135 Ack: Do you acknowledge this as your signature and your free act and deed, for the purposes stated herein?
Jurat: Do you solemnly (swear/affirm) that this statement is true, (so help you God / on your honor)?

Signer 1 Name and Address:

Signer 2 Name and Address:

Identification Method: ☐ Personally Known ☐ Other
☐ Texas Driver's License ☐ Driver's License ☐ Passport

Identification Method: ☐ Personally Known ☐ Other
☐ Texas Driver's License ☐ Driver's License ☐ Passport

Sign Here

Sign Here

X _____

X _____

Date/Time: _____   Ref#: _____

Signing Address:

Document Date	Notarization Ack Jur Oth Fee if any	Document Description	Signer Initials	
			1	2
		Deed of Trust / Mortgage		
		Deed - General - Quit Claim - Special Warranty		
		Borrower's Title Affidavit		
		Borrower's Closing Affidavit		
		E&O / Compliance Agreement		
		Occupancy Affidavit		
		Signature Name Affidavit		
		Power of Attorney - Limited / Durable		
		T-47 Residential Real Property Affidavit		
		Mineral Rights Acknowledgement and Agreement		

Document
Designation of Homestead / Non-Homestead
Notice of Penalties for Making False or Misleading Statements
Ownership Affidavit
Occupancy and Financial Status Affidavit
Obligation of Debts Affidavit
Release of Claims and Hold Harmless Agreement
Affidavit of Marital Status
Tax Indemnity
Compliance / Correction Agreement

Notes:

Ack: Do you acknowledge this as your signature and your free act and deed, for the purposes stated herein?

Jurat: Do you solemnly (swear/affirm) that this statement is true, (so help you God / on your honor)?

| Signer 1 Name and Address: | | Signer 2 Name and Address: | |

Identification Method: ☐ Personally Known ☐ Other
☐ Texas Driver's License ☐ Driver's License ☐ Passport

Identification Method: ☐ Personally Known ☐ Other
☐ Texas Driver's License ☐ Driver's License ☐ Passport

Sign Here

Sign Here

X _____

X _____ Ref#:

Date/Time:

Signing Address:

Document Date	Notarization **Ack Jur Oth** Fee if any	Document Description	Signer Initials	
			1	2
		Deed of Trust / Mortgage		
		Deed - General - Quit Claim - Special Warranty		
		Borrower's Title Affidavit		
		Borrower's Closing Affidavit		
		E&O / Compliance Agreement		
		Occupancy Affidavit		
		Signature Name Affidavit		
		Power of Attorney - Limited / Durable		
		T-47 Residential Real Property Affidavit		
		Mineral Rights Acknowledgement and Agreement		

Designation of Homestead / Non-Homestead					
Notice of Penalties for Making False or Misleading Statements					
Ownership Affidavit					
Occupancy and Financial Status Affidavit					
Obligation of Debts Affidavit					
Release of Claims and Hold Harmless Agreement					
Affidavit of Marital Status					
Tax Indemnity					
Compliance / Correction Agreement					

Notes:

139 Ack: Do you acknowledge this as your signature and your free act and deed, for the purposes stated herein?
Jurat: Do you solemnly (swear/affirm) that this statement is true, (so help you God / on your honor)?

Signer 1 Name and Address:		Signer 2 Name and Address:	
Identification Method: ☐ Personally Known ☐ Other ☐ Texas Driver's License ☐ Driver's License ☐ Passport		**Identification Method:** ☐ Personally Known ☐ Other ☐ Texas Driver's License ☐ Driver's License ☐ Passport	

Sign Here

Sign Here

X _____

X _____

Date/Time: _____   **Ref#:** _____

Signing Address:

Document Date	Notarization **A**ck **J**ur **O**th Fee if any	Document Description	Signer Initials	
			1	2
		Deed of Trust / Mortgage		
		Deed - General - Quit Claim - Special Warranty		
		Borrower's Title Affidavit		
		Borrower's Closing Affidavit		
		E&O / Compliance Agreement		
		Occupancy Affidavit		
		Signature Name Affidavit		
		Power of Attorney - Limited / Durable		
		T-47 Residential Real Property Affidavit		
		Mineral Rights Acknowledgement and Agreement		

Designation of Homestead / Non-Homestead																	
Notice of Penalties for Making False or Misleading Statements																	
Ownership Affidavit																	
Occupancy and Financial Status Affidavit																	
Obligation of Debts Affidavit																	
Release of Claims and Hold Harmless Agreement																	
Affidavit of Marital Status																	
Tax Indemnity																	
Compliance / Correction Agreement																	

Notes:

141 Ack:Do you acknowledge this as your signature and your free act and deed, for the purposes stated herein?
Jurat: Do you solemnly (swear/affirm) that this statement is true, (so help you God / on your honor)?

| Signer 1 Name and Address: | | Signer 2 Name and Address: | |

Identification Method: ☐ Personally Known ☐ Other
☐ Texas Driver's License ☐ Driver's License ☐ Passport

Identification Method: ☐ Personally Known ☐ Other
☐ Texas Driver's License ☐ Driver's License ☐ Passport

Sign Here

X _____

Sign Here

X _____

Date/Time: **Ref#:**

Signing Address:

Document Date	Notarization Ack Jur Oth Fee if any	Document Description	Signer Initials	
			1	2
		Deed of Trust / Mortgage		
		Deed - General - Quit Claim - Special Warranty		
		Borrower's Title Affidavit		
		Borrower's Closing Affidavit		
		E&O / Compliance Agreement		
		Occupancy Affidavit		
		Signature Name Affidavit		
		Power of Attorney - Limited / Durable		
		T-47 Residential Real Property Affidavit		
		Mineral Rights Acknowledgement and Agreement		

	Designation of Homestead / Non-Homestead
	Notice of Penalties for Making False or Misleading Statements
	Ownership Affidavit
	Occupancy and Financial Status Affidavit
	Obligation of Debts Affidavit
	Release of Claims and Hold Harmless Agreement
	Affidavit of Marital Status
	Tax Indemnity
	Compliance / Correction Agreement

Notes:

143 Ack:Do you acknowledge this as your signature and your free act and deed, for the purposes stated herein?
Jurat: Do you solemnly (swear/affirm) that this statement is true, (so help you God / on your honor)?

| Signer 1 Name and Address: | | Signer 2 Name and Address: | |

Signer 1 Name and Address:

Identification Method: ☐ Personally Known ☐ Other
☐ Texas Driver's License ☐ Driver's License ☐ Passport

Signer 2 Name and Address:

Identification Method: ☐ Personally Known ☐ Other
☐ Texas Driver's License ☐ Driver's License ☐ Passport

Sign Here

Sign Here

X _____

X _____

Ref#: _____

Date/Time:

Signing Address:

Document Date	Notarization **A**ck **J**ur **O**th Fee if any	Document Description	Signer Initials	
			1	2
		Deed of Trust / Mortgage		
		Deed - General - Quit Claim - Special Warranty		
		Borrower's Title Affidavit		
		Borrower's Closing Affidavit		
		E&O / Compliance Agreement		
		Occupancy Affidavit		
		Signature Name Affidavit		
		Power of Attorney - Limited / Durable		
		T-47 Residential Real Property Affidavit		
		Mineral Rights Acknowledgement and Agreement		

	Designation of Homestead / Non-Homestead
	Notice of Penalties for Making False or Misleading Statements
	Ownership Affidavit
	Occupancy and Financial Status Affidavit
	Obligation of Debts Affidavit
	Release of Claims and Hold Harmless Agreement
	Affidavit of Marital Status
	Tax Indemnity
	Compliance / Correction Agreement

Notes:

145 Ack: Do you acknowledge this as your signature and your free act and deed, for the purposes stated herein?
Jurat: Do you solemnly (swear/affirm) that this statement is true, (so help you God / on your honor)?

Signer 1 Name
and Address:

Signer 2 Name
and Address:

Identification Method: ☐ Personally Known ☐ Other
☐ Texas Driver's License ☐ Driver's License ☐ Passport

Identification Method: ☐ Personally Known ☐ Other
☐ Texas Driver's License ☐ Driver's License ☐ Passport

Sign Here

Sign Here

X _____

X _____

Date/Time: Ref#:

Signing Address:

Document Date	Notarization Ack Jur Oth Fee if any	Document Description	Signer Initials	
			1	2
		Deed of Trust / Mortgage		
		Deed - General - Quit Claim - Special Warranty		
		Borrower's Title Affidavit		
		Borrower's Closing Affidavit		
		E&O / Compliance Agreement		
		Occupancy Affidavit		
		Signature Name Affidavit		
		Power of Attorney - Limited / Durable		
		T-47 Residential Real Property Affidavit		
		Mineral Rights Acknowledgement and Agreement		

	Designation of Homestead / Non-Homestead
	Notice of Penalties for Making False or Misleading Statements
	Ownership Affidavit
	Occupancy and Financial Status Affidavit
	Obligation of Debts Affidavit
	Release of Claims and Hold Harmless Agreement
	Affidavit of Marital Status
	Tax Indemnity
	Compliance / Correction Agreement

Notes:

Ack: Do you acknowledge this as your signature and your free act and deed, for the purposes stated herein?
Jurat: Do you solemnly (swear/affirm) that this statement is true, (so help you God / on your honor)?

| Signer 1 Name and Address: | | Signer 2 Name and Address: | |

Identification Method: ☐ Personally Known ☐ Other
☐ Texas Driver's License ☐ Driver's License ☐ Passport

Identification Method: ☐ Personally Known ☐ Other
☐ Texas Driver's License ☐ Driver's License ☐ Passport

Sign Here

X _____

Sign Here

X _____

Date/Time: _____ **Ref#:** _____

Signing Address:

Document Date	Notarization **Ack Jur Oth** Fee if any	Document Description	Signer Initials	
			1	2
		Deed of Trust / Mortgage		
		Deed - General - Quit Claim - Special Warranty		
		Borrower's Title Affidavit		
		Borrower's Closing Affidavit		
		E&O / Compliance Agreement		
		Occupancy Affidavit		
		Signature Name Affidavit		
		Power of Attorney - Limited / Durable		
		T-47 Residential Real Property Affidavit		
		Mineral Rights Acknowledgement and Agreement		

			Designation of Homestead / Non-Homestead			
			Notice of Penalties for Making False or Misleading Statements			
			Ownership Affidavit			
			Occupancy and Financial Status Affidavit			
			Obligation of Debts Affidavit			
			Release of Claims and Hold Harmless Agreement			
			Affidavit of Marital Status			
			Tax Indemnity			
			Compliance / Correction Agreement			

Notes:

149 Ack: Do you acknowledge this as your signature and your free act and deed, for the purposes stated herein?
Jurat: Do you solemnly (swear/affirm) that this statement is true, (so help you God / on your honor)?

Signer 1 Name and Address:		Signer 2 Name and Address:	

Identification Method: ☐ Personally Known ☐ Other
☐ Texas Driver's License ☐ Driver's License ☐ Passport

Identification Method: ☐ Personally Known ☐ Other
☐ Texas Driver's License ☐ Driver's License ☐ Passport

Sign Here

X _____

Sign Here

X _____ Ref#: _____

Date/Time:

Signing Address:

Document Date	Notarization Ack **J**ur **O**th Fee if any	Document Description	Signer Initials	
			1	2
		Deed of Trust / Mortgage		
		Deed - General - Quit Claim - Special Warranty		
		Borrower's Title Affidavit		
		Borrower's Closing Affidavit		
		E&O / Compliance Agreement		
		Occupancy Affidavit		
		Signature Name Affidavit		
		Power of Attorney - Limited / Durable		
		T-47 Residential Real Property Affidavit		
		Mineral Rights Acknowledgement and Agreement		

		Designation of Homestead / Non-Homestead	Notice of Penalties for Making False or Misleading Statements		Ownership Affidavit	Occupancy and Financial Status Affidavit		Obligation of Debts Affidavit	Release of Claims and Hold Harmless Agreement		Affidavit of Marital Status	Tax Indemnity	Compliance / Correction Agreement								

Notes:

151 Ack:Do you acknowledge this as your signature and your free act and deed, for the purposes stated herein?
Jurat: Do you solemnly (swear/affirm) that this statement is true, (so help you God / on your honor)?

| Signer 1 Name and Address: | | | Signer 2 Name and Address: | |

Identification Method: ☐ Personally Known ☐ Other
☐ Texas Driver's License ☐ Driver's License ☐ Passport

Identification Method: ☐ Personally Known ☐ Other
☐ Texas Driver's License ☐ Driver's License ☐ Passport

Sign Here

X _____

Sign Here

X _____

Date/Time: _____   **Ref#:** _____

Signing Address:

Document Date	Notarization Ack Jur Oth Fee if any	Document Description	Signer Initials	
			1	2
		Deed of Trust / Mortgage		
		Deed - General - Quit Claim - Special Warranty		
		Borrower's Title Affidavit		
		Borrower's Closing Affidavit		
		E&O / Compliance Agreement		
		Occupancy Affidavit		
		Signature Name Affidavit		
		Power of Attorney - Limited / Durable		
		T-47 Residential Real Property Affidavit		
		Mineral Rights Acknowledgement and Agreement		

Document		
Designation of Homestead / Non-Homestead		
Notice of Penalties for Making False or Misleading Statements		
Ownership Affidavit		
Occupancy and Financial Status Affidavit		
Obligation of Debts Affidavit		
Release of Claims and Hold Harmless Agreement		
Affidavit of Marital Status		
Tax Indemnity		
Compliance / Correction Agreement		

Notes:

153 Ack: Do you acknowledge this as your signature and your free act and deed, for the purposes stated herein?
Jurat: Do you solemnly (swear/affirm) that this statement is true, (so help you God / on your honor)?

| Signer 1 Name and Address: | | Signer 2 Name and Address: | |

Signer 1 Name and Address:

Identification Method: ☐ Personally Known ☐ Other
☐ Texas Driver's License ☐ Driver's License ☐ Passport

Sign Here

X _____

Date/Time: _____

Signing Address:

Signer 2 Name and Address:

Identification Method: ☐ Personally Known ☐ Other
☐ Texas Driver's License ☐ Driver's License ☐ Passport

Sign Here

X _____

Ref#: _____

Document Date	Notarization Ack **J**ur **O**th Fee if any	Document Description	Signer Initials	
			1	2
		Deed of Trust / Mortgage		
		Deed – General – Quit Claim – Special Warranty		
		Borrower's Title Affidavit		
		Borrower's Closing Affidavit		
		E&O / Compliance Agreement		
		Occupancy Affidavit		
		Signature Name Affidavit		
		Power of Attorney – Limited / Durable		
		T-47 Residential Real Property Affidavit		
		Mineral Rights Acknowledgement and Agreement		

		Designation of Homestead / Non-Homestead	Notice of Penalties for Making False or Misleading Statements	Ownership Affidavit	Occupancy and Financial Status Affidavit	Obligation of Debts Affidavit	Release of Claims and Hold Harmless Agreement	Affidavit of Marital Status	Tax Indemnity	Compliance / Correction Agreement									

Notes:

155 Ack: Do you acknowledge this as your signature and your free act and deed, for the purposes stated herein?
Jurat: Do you solemnly (swear/affirm) that this statement is true, (so help you God / on your honor)?

Signer 1 Name and Address:		Signer 2 Name and Address:	
Identification Method:☐ Personally Known ☐ Other ☐ Texas Driver's License ☐ Driver's License ☐ Passport		Identification Method:☐ Personally Known ☐ Other ☐ Texas Driver's License ☐ Driver's License ☐ Passport	

Sign Here

X _____

Sign Here

X _____

Date/Time: _____   Ref# :

Signing Address:

Document Date	Notarization **A**ck **J**ur **O**th Fee if any	Document Description	Signer Initials	
			1	2
		Deed of Trust / Mortgage		
		Deed - General - Quit Claim - Special Warranty		
		Borrower's Title Affidavit		
		Borrower's Closing Affidavit		
		E&O / Compliance Agreement		
		Occupancy Affidavit		
		Signature Name Affidavit		
		Power of Attorney - Limited / Durable		
		T-47 Residential Real Property Affidavit		
		Mineral Rights Acknowledgement and Agreement		

	Designation of Homestead / Non-Homestead
	Notice of Penalties for Making False or Misleading Statements
	Ownership Affidavit
	Occupancy and Financial Status Affidavit
	Obligation of Debts Affidavit
	Release of Claims and Hold Harmless Agreement
	Affidavit of Marital Status
	Tax Indemnity
	Compliance / Correction Agreement

Notes:

157 Ack: Do you acknowledge this as your signature and your free act and deed, for the purposes stated herein?
Jurat: Do you solemnly (swear/affirm) that this statement is true, (so help you God / on your honor)?

Signer 1 Name and Address:		Signer 2 Name and Address:	

Identification Method: ☐ Personally Known ☐ Other
☐ Texas Driver's License ☐ Driver's License ☐ Passport

Identification Method: ☐ Personally Known ☐ Other
☐ Texas Driver's License ☐ Driver's License ☐ Passport

Sign Here

Sign Here

X _____

X _____

Date/Time: _____ Ref #: _____

Signing Address:

Document Date	Notarization Ack **J**ur **O**th Fee if any	Document Description	Signer Initials	
			1	2
		Deed of Trust / Mortgage		
		Deed - General - Quit Claim - Special Warranty		
		Borrower's Title Affidavit		
		Borrower's Closing Affidavit		
		E&O / Compliance Agreement		
		Occupancy Affidavit		
		Signature Name Affidavit		
		Power of Attorney - Limited / Durable		
		T-47 Residential Real Property Affidavit		
		Mineral Rights Acknowledgement and Agreement		

Designation of Homestead / Non-Homestead	
Notice of Penalties for Making False or Misleading Statements	
Ownership Affidavit	
Occupancy and Financial Status Affidavit	
Obligation of Debts Affidavit	
Release of Claims and Hold Harmless Agreement	
Affidavit of Marital Status	
Tax Indemnity	
Compliance / Correction Agreement	

Notes:

Ack:Do you acknowledge this as your signature and your free act and deed, for the purposes stated herein?
Jurat: Do you solemnly (swear/affirm) that this statement is true, (so help you God / on your honor)?

Signer 1 Name and Address:

Signer 2 Name and Address:

Identification Method: ☐ Personally Known ☐ Other
☐ Texas Driver's License ☐ Driver's License ☐ Passport

Identification Method: ☐ Personally Known ☐ Other
☐ Texas Driver's License ☐ Driver's License ☐ Passport

Sign Here

Sign Here

X _____

X _____

Date/Time:

Ref#:

Signing Address:

Document Date	Notarization Ack Jur Oth Fee if any	Document Description	Signer Initials	
			1	2
		Deed of Trust / Mortgage		
		Deed - General - Quit Claim - Special Warranty		
		Borrower's Title Affidavit		
		Borrower's Closing Affidavit		
		E&O / Compliance Agreement		
		Occupancy Affidavit		
		Signature Name Affidavit		
		Power of Attorney - Limited / Durable		
		T-47 Residential Real Property Affidavit		
		Mineral Rights Acknowledgement and Agreement		

		Designation of Homestead / Non-Homestead													
		Notice of Penalties for Making False or Misleading Statements													
		Ownership Affidavit													
		Occupancy and Financial Status Affidavit													
		Obligation of Debts Affidavit													
		Release of Claims and Hold Harmless Agreement													
		Affidavit of Marital Status													
		Tax Indemnity													
		Compliance / Correction Agreement													

Notes:

161 Ack: Do you acknowledge this as your signature and your free act and deed, for the purposes stated herein?
Jurat: Do you solemnly (swear/affirm) that this statement is true, (so help you God / on your honor)?

Signer 1 Name and Address:			Signer 2 Name and Address:	

Identification Method: ☐ Personally Known ☐ Other
☐ Texas Driver's License ☐ Driver's License ☐ Passport

Identification Method: ☐ Personally Known ☐ Other
☐ Texas Driver's License ☐ Driver's License ☐ Passport

Sign Here

Sign Here

X _____

X _____

Date/Time:

Ref #:

Signing Address:

Document Date	Notarization Ack Jur Oth Fee if any	Document Description	Signer Initials	
			1	2
		Deed of Trust / Mortgage		
		Deed - General - Quit Claim - Special Warranty		
		Borrower's Title Affidavit		
		Borrower's Closing Affidavit		
		E&O / Compliance Agreement		
		Occupancy Affidavit		
		Signature Name Affidavit		
		Power of Attorney - Limited / Durable		
		T-47 Residential Real Property Affidavit		
		Mineral Rights Acknowledgement and Agreement		

Designation of Homestead / Non-Homestead	
Notice of Penalties for Making False or Misleading Statements	
Ownership Affidavit	
Occupancy and Financial Status Affidavit	
Obligation of Debts Affidavit	
Release of Claims and Hold Harmless Agreement	
Affidavit of Marital Status	
Tax Indemnity	
Compliance / Correction Agreement	

Notes:

163 Ack:Do you acknowledge this as your signature and your free act and deed, for the purposes stated herein?
Jurat: Do you solemnly (swear/affirm) that this statement is true, (so help you God / on your honor)?

| Signer 1 Name and Address: | | Signer 2 Name and Address: | | |

Signer 1 Name and Address:

Identification Method: ☐ Personally Known ☐ Other
☐ Texas Driver's License ☐ Driver's License ☐ Passport

X _____

Sign Here

Date/Time: _____

Signing Address:

Signer 2 Name and Address:

Identification Method: ☐ Personally Known ☐ Other
☐ Texas Driver's License ☐ Driver's License ☐ Passport

X _____

Sign Here

Ref#: _____

Document Date	Notarization **Ack Jur Oth** Fee if any	Document Description	Signer Initials	
			1	2
		Deed of Trust / Mortgage		
		Deed – General – Quit Claim – Special Warranty		
		Borrower's Title Affidavit		
		Borrower's Closing Affidavit		
		E&O / Compliance Agreement		
		Occupancy Affidavit		
		Signature Name Affidavit		
		Power of Attorney – Limited / Durable		
		T-47 Residential Real Property Affidavit		
		Mineral Rights Acknowledgement and Agreement		

Designation of Homestead / Non-Homestead	
Notice of Penalties for Making False or Misleading Statements	
Ownership Affidavit	
Occupancy and Financial Status Affidavit	
Obligation of Debts Affidavit	
Release of Claims and Hold Harmless Agreement	
Affidavit of Marital Status	
Tax Indemnity	
Compliance / Correction Agreement	

Notes:

165 Ack: Do you acknowledge this as your signature and your free act and deed, for the purposes stated herein?
Jurat: Do you solemnly (swear/affirm) that this statement is true, (so help you God / on your honor)?

Signer 1 Name
and Address:

Signer 2 Name
and Address:

Identification Method:☐ Personally Known ☐ Other
☐ Texas Driver's License ☐ Driver's License ☐ Passport

Identification Method:☐ Personally Known ☐ Other
☐ Texas Driver's License ☐ Driver's License ☐ Passport

Sign Here

Sign Here

X _____

X _____

Date/Time:

Ref#:

Signing Address:

Document Date	Notarization Ack **J**ur **O**th Fee if any	Document Description	Signer Initials	
			1	2
		Deed of Trust / Mortgage		
		Deed - General - Quit Claim - Special Warranty		
		Borrower's Title Affidavit		
		Borrower's Closing Affidavit		
		E&O / Compliance Agreement		
		Occupancy Affidavit		
		Signature Name Affidavit		
		Power of Attorney - Limited / Durable		
		T-47 Residential Real Property Affidavit		
		Mineral Rights Acknowledgement and Agreement		

	Designation of Homestead / Non-Homestead
	Notice of Penalties for Making False or Misleading Statements
	Ownership Affidavit
	Occupancy and Financial Status Affidavit
	Obligation of Debts Affidavit
	Release of Claims and Hold Harmless Agreement
	Affidavit of Marital Status
	Tax Indemnity
	Compliance / Correction Agreement

Notes:

Ack: Do you acknowledge this as your signature and your free act and deed, for the purposes stated herein?
Jurat: Do you solemnly (swear/affirm) that this statement is true, (so help you God / on your honor)?

| Signer 1 Name and Address: | | Signer 2 Name and Address: | |

Identification Method: ☐ Personally Known ☐ Other
☐ Texas Driver's License ☐ Driver's License ☐ Passport

Identification Method: ☐ Personally Known ☐ Other
☐ Texas Driver's License ☐ Driver's License ☐ Passport

Sign Here

Sign Here

X _____

X _____

Date/Time: _____   Ref#: _____

Signing Address:

Document Date	Notarization Ack Jur Oth Fee if any	Document Description	Signer Initials	
			1	2
		Deed of Trust / Mortgage		
		Deed - General - Quit Claim - Special Warranty		
		Borrower's Title Affidavit		
		Borrower's Closing Affidavit		
		E&O / Compliance Agreement		
		Occupancy Affidavit		
		Signature Name Affidavit		
		Power of Attorney - Limited / Durable		
		T-47 Residential Real Property Affidavit		
		Mineral Rights Acknowledgement and Agreement		

		Designation of Homestead / Non-Homestead
		Notice of Penalties for Making False or Misleading Statements
		Ownership Affidavit
		Occupancy and Financial Status Affidavit
		Obligation of Debts Affidavit
		Release of Claims and Hold Harmless Agreement
		Affidavit of Marital Status
		Tax Indemnity
		Compliance / Correction Agreement

Notes:

169 Ack:Do you acknowledge this as your signature and your free act and deed, for the purposes stated herein?
Jurat: Do you solemnly (swear/affirm) that this statement is true, (so help you God / on your honor)?

Signer 1 Name and Address:

Identification Method: ☐ Personally Known ☐ Other
☐ Texas Driver's License ☐ Driver's License ☐ Passport

Sign Here

X _____

Date/Time: _____

Signing Address:

Signer 2 Name and Address:

Identification Method: ☐ Personally Known ☐ Other
☐ Texas Driver's License ☐ Driver's License ☐ Passport

Sign Here

X _____

Ref#: _____

Document Date	Notarization Ack Jur Oth Fee if any	Document Description	Signer Initials	
			1	2
		Deed of Trust / Mortgage		
		Deed - General - Quit Claim - Special Warranty		
		Borrower's Title Affidavit		
		Borrower's Closing Affidavit		
		E&O / Compliance Agreement		
		Occupancy Affidavit		
		Signature Name Affidavit		
		Power of Attorney - Limited / Durable		
		T-47 Residential Real Property Affidavit		
		Mineral Rights Acknowledgement and Agreement		

Designation of Homestead / Non-Homestead		
Notice of Penalties for Making False or Misleading Statements		
Ownership Affidavit		
Occupancy and Financial Status Affidavit		
Obligation of Debts Affidavit		
Release of Claims and Hold Harmless Agreement		
Affidavit of Marital Status		
Tax Indemnity		
Compliance / Correction Agreement		

Notes:

Ack: Do you acknowledge this as your signature and your free act and deed, for the purposes stated herein?
Jurat: Do you solemnly (swear/affirm) that this statement is true, (so help you God / on your honor)?

| Signer 1 Name and Address: | | Signer 2 Name and Address: | |

Signer 1 Name and Address:

Identification Method: ☐ Personally Known ☐ Other
☐ Texas Driver's License ☐ Driver's License ☐ Passport

Sign Here

X _____

Date/Time: _____

Signing Address:

Signer 2 Name and Address:

Identification Method: ☐ Personally Known ☐ Other
☐ Texas Driver's License ☐ Driver's License ☐ Passport

Sign Here

X _____

Ref#: _____

Document Date	Notarization Ack **J**ur **O**th Fee if any	Document Description	Signer Initials	
			1	2
		Deed of Trust / Mortgage		
		Deed - General - Quit Claim - Special Warranty		
		Borrower's Title Affidavit		
		Borrower's Closing Affidavit		
		E&O / Compliance Agreement		
		Occupancy Affidavit		
		Signature Name Affidavit		
		Power of Attorney - Limited / Durable		
		T-47 Residential Real Property Affidavit		
		Mineral Rights Acknowledgement and Agreement		

Designation of Homestead / Non-Homestead	
Notice of Penalties for Making False or Misleading Statements	
Ownership Affidavit	
Occupancy and Financial Status Affidavit	
Obligation of Debts Affidavit	
Release of Claims and Hold Harmless Agreement	
Affidavit of Marital Status	
Tax Indemnity	
Compliance / Correction Agreement	

Notes:

173 Ack: Do you acknowledge this as your signature and your free act and deed, for the purposes stated herein?
Jurat: Do you solemnly (swear/affirm) that this statement is true, (so help you God / on your honor)?

| Signer 1 Name and Address: | | Signer 2 Name and Address: | |

Signer 1 Name and Address:

Identification Method: ☐ Personally Known ☐ Other
☐ Texas Driver's License ☐ Driver's License ☐ Passport

Signer 2 Name and Address:

Identification Method: ☐ Personally Known ☐ Other
☐ Texas Driver's License ☐ Driver's License ☐ Passport

Sign Here

X _____

Sign Here

X _____

Date/Time:

Ref#:

Signing Address:

Document Date	Notarization Ack Jur Oth Fee if any	Document Description	Signer Initials	
			1	2
		Deed of Trust / Mortgage		
		Deed - General - Quit Claim - Special Warranty		
		Borrower's Title Affidavit		
		Borrower's Closing Affidavit		
		E&O / Compliance Agreement		
		Occupancy Affidavit		
		Signature Name Affidavit		
		Power of Attorney - Limited / Durable		
		T-47 Residential Real Property Affidavit		
		Mineral Rights Acknowledgement and Agreement		

	Designation of Homestead / Non-Homestead
	Notice of Penalties for Making False or Misleading Statements
	Ownership Affidavit
	Occupancy and Financial Status Affidavit
	Obligation of Debts Affidavit
	Release of Claims and Hold Harmless Agreement
	Affidavit of Marital Status
	Tax Indemnity
	Compliance / Correction Agreement

Notes:

175 Ack: Do you acknowledge this as your signature and your free act and deed, for the purposes stated herein?
Jurat: Do you solemnly (swear/affirm) that this statement is true, (so help you God / on your honor)?

| Signer 1 Name and Address: | | Signer 2 Name and Address: | |

Identification Method: ☐ Personally Known ☐ Other
☐ Texas Driver's License ☐ Driver's License ☐ Passport

Identification Method: ☐ Personally Known ☐ Other
☐ Texas Driver's License ☐ Driver's License ☐ Passport

Sign Here

Sign Here

X _____

X _____

Date/Time: _____ Ref#: _____

Signing Address:

Document Date	Notarization Ack Jur Oth Fee if any	Document Description	Signer Initials	
			1	2
		Deed of Trust / Mortgage		
		Deed - General - Quit Claim - Special Warranty		
		Borrower's Title Affidavit		
		Borrower's Closing Affidavit		
		E&O / Compliance Agreement		
		Occupancy Affidavit		
		Signature Name Affidavit		
		Power of Attorney - Limited / Durable		
		T-47 Residential Real Property Affidavit		
		Mineral Rights Acknowledgement and Agreement		

Designation of Homestead / Non-Homestead		
Notice of Penalties for Making False or Misleading Statements		
Ownership Affidavit		
Occupancy and Financial Status Affidavit		
Obligation of Debts Affidavit		
Release of Claims and Hold Harmless Agreement		
Affidavit of Marital Status		
Tax Indemnity		
Compliance / Correction Agreement		

Notes:

Ack:Do you acknowledge this as your signature and your free act and deed, for the purposes stated herein?
Jurat: Do you solemnly (swear/affirm) that this statement is true, (so help you God / on your honor)?

Signer 1 Name and Address:		Signer 2 Name and Address:	

Identification Method: ☐ Personally Known ☐ Other ☐ Texas Driver's License ☐ Driver's License ☐ Passport	Identification Method: ☐ Personally Known ☐ Other ☐ Texas Driver's License ☐ Driver's License ☐ Passport

Sign Here

X _____   X _____

Date/Time: _____   **Ref#:** _____

Signing Address:

Document Date	Notarization **A**ck **J**ur **O**th Fee if any	Document Description	Signer Initials	
			1	2
		Deed of Trust / Mortgage		
		Deed - General - Quit Claim - Special Warranty		
		Borrower's Title Affidavit		
		Borrower's Closing Affidavit		
		E&O / Compliance Agreement		
		Occupancy Affidavit		
		Signature Name Affidavit		
		Power of Attorney - Limited / Durable		
		T-47 Residential Real Property Affidavit		
		Mineral Rights Acknowledgement and Agreement		

		Designation of Homestead / Non-Homestead	Notice of Penalties for Making False or Misleading Statements	Ownership Affidavit	Occupancy and Financial Status Affidavit	Obligation of Debts Affidavit	Release of Claims and Hold Harmless Agreement	Affidavit of Marital Status	Tax Indemnity	Compliance / Correction Agreement								

Notes:

Ack: Do you acknowledge this as your signature and your free act and deed, for the purposes stated herein?
Jurat: Do you solemnly (swear/affirm) that this statement is true, (so help you God / on your honor)?

Signer 1 Name and Address:		Signer 2 Name and Address:	
Identification Method:☐ Personally Known ☐ Other ☐ Texas Driver's License ☐ Driver's License ☐ Passport		Identification Method:☐ Personally Known ☐ Other ☐ Texas Driver's License ☐ Driver's License ☐ Passport	

Sign Here

Sign Here

X _____

X _____

Date/Time: Ref#:

Signing Address:

Document Date	Notarization **Ack Jur Oth** Fee if any	Document Description	Signer Initials	
			1	2
		Deed of Trust / Mortgage		
		Deed - General - Quit Claim - Special Warranty		
		Borrower's Title Affidavit		
		Borrower's Closing Affidavit		
		E&O / Compliance Agreement		
		Occupancy Affidavit		
		Signature Name Affidavit		
		Power of Attorney - Limited / Durable		
		T-47 Residential Real Property Affidavit		
		Mineral Rights Acknowledgement and Agreement		

Designation of Homestead / Non-Homestead						
Notice of Penalties for Making False or Misleading Statements						
Ownership Affidavit						
Occupancy and Financial Status Affidavit						
Obligation of Debts Affidavit						
Release of Claims and Hold Harmless Agreement						
Affidavit of Marital Status						
Tax Indemnity						
Compliance / Correction Agreement						

Notes:

181 Ack: Do you acknowledge this as your signature and your free act and deed, for the purposes stated herein?
Jurat: Do you solemnly (swear/affirm) that this statement is true, (so help you God / on your honor)?

| Signer 1 Name and Address: | | Signer 2 Name and Address: | |

Identification Method: ☐ Personally Known ☐ Other
☐ Texas Driver's License ☐ Driver's License ☐ Passport

Identification Method: ☐ Personally Known ☐ Other
☐ Texas Driver's License ☐ Driver's License ☐ Passport

Sign Here

X _____

Sign Here

X _____

Date/Time:

Ref#:

Signing Address:

Document Date	Notarization Ack **J**ur **O**th Fee if any	Document Description	Signer Initials	
			1	2
		Deed of Trust / Mortgage		
		Deed - General - Quit Claim - Special Warranty		
		Borrower's Title Affidavit		
		Borrower's Closing Affidavit		
		E&O / Compliance Agreement		
		Occupancy Affidavit		
		Signature Name Affidavit		
		Power of Attorney - Limited / Durable		
		T-47 Residential Real Property Affidavit		
		Mineral Rights Acknowledgement and Agreement		

			Designation of Homestead / Non-Homestead			
			Notice of Penalties for Making False or Misleading Statements			
			Ownership Affidavit			
			Occupancy and Financial Status Affidavit			
			Obligation of Debts Affidavit			
			Release of Claims and Hold Harmless Agreement			
			Affidavit of Marital Status			
			Tax Indemnity			
			Compliance / Correction Agreement			

Notes:

183 Ack: Do you acknowledge this as your signature and your free act and deed, for the purposes stated herein?
Jurat: Do you solemnly (swear/affirm) that this statement is true, (so help you God / on your honor)?

Signer 1 Name
and Address:

Signer 2 Name
and Address:

Identification Method: ☐ Personally Known   ☐ Other
☐ Texas Driver's License ☐ Driver's License ☐ Passport

Identification Method: ☐ Personally Known   ☐ Other
☐ Texas Driver's License ☐ Driver's License ☐ Passport

Sign Here

Sign Here

X _____

X _____

Date/Time:

Ref#:

Signing Address:

Document Date	Notarization **Ack Jur Oth** Fee if any	Document Description	Signer Initials	
			1	2
		Deed of Trust / Mortgage		
		Deed - General - Quit Claim - Special Warranty		
		Borrower's Title Affidavit		
		Borrower's Closing Affidavit		
		E&O / Compliance Agreement		
		Occupancy Affidavit		
		Signature Name Affidavit		
		Power of Attorney - Limited / Durable		
		T-47 Residential Real Property Affidavit		
		Mineral Rights Acknowledgement and Agreement		

		Designation of Homestead / Non-Homestead
		Notice of Penalties for Making False or Misleading Statements
		Ownership Affidavit
		Occupancy and Financial Status Affidavit
		Obligation of Debts Affidavit
		Release of Claims and Hold Harmless Agreement
		Affidavit of Marital Status
		Tax Indemnity
		Compliance / Correction Agreement

Notes:

185 Ack: Do you acknowledge this as your signature and your free act and deed, for the purposes stated herein?
Jurat: Do you solemnly (swear/affirm) that this statement is true, (so help you God / on your honor)?

| Signer 1 Name and Address: | | Signer 2 Name and Address: | |

Identification Method: ☐ Personally Known ☐ Other
☐ Texas Driver's License ☐ Driver's License ☐ Passport

Identification Method: ☐ Personally Known ☐ Other
☐ Texas Driver's License ☐ Driver's License ☐ Passport

Sign Here

X _____

X _____

Date/Time: _____   Ref#: _____

Signing Address: _____

Document Date	Notarization Ack Jur Oth Fee if any	Document Description	Signer Initials	
			1	2
		Deed of Trust / Mortgage		
		Deed - General - Quit Claim - Special Warranty		
		Borrower's Title Affidavit		
		Borrower's Closing Affidavit		
		E&O / Compliance Agreement		
		Occupancy Affidavit		
		Signature Name Affidavit		
		Power of Attorney - Limited / Durable		
		T-47 Residential Real Property Affidavit		
		Mineral Rights Acknowledgement and Agreement		

	Designation of Homestead / Non-Homestead
	Notice of Penalties for Making False or Misleading Statements
	Ownership Affidavit
	Occupancy and Financial Status Affidavit
	Obligation of Debts Affidavit
	Release of Claims and Hold Harmless Agreement
	Affidavit of Marital Status
	Tax Indemnity
	Compliance / Correction Agreement

Notes:

Ack:Do you acknowledge this as your signature and your free act and deed, for the purposes stated herein?
Jurat: Do you solemnly (swear/affirm) that this statement is true, (so help you God / on your honor)?

Signer 1 Name and Address:

Identification Method: ☐ Personally Known ☐ Other
☐ Texas Driver's License ☐ Driver's License ☐ Passport

Sign Here

X _____

Date/Time:

Signing Address:

Signer 2 Name and Address:

Identification Method: ☐ Personally Known ☐ Other
☐ Texas Driver's License ☐ Driver's License ☐ Passport

Sign Here

X _____

Ref # :

Document Date	Notarization **Ack Jur Oth** Fee if any	Document Description	Signer Initials	
			1	2
		Deed of Trust / Mortgage		
		Deed - General - Quit Claim - Special Warranty		
		Borrower's Title Affidavit		
		Borrower's Closing Affidavit		
		E&O / Compliance Agreement		
		Occupancy Affidavit		
		Signature Name Affidavit		
		Power of Attorney - Limited / Durable		
		T-47 Residential Real Property Affidavit		
		Mineral Rights Acknowledgement and Agreement		

		Designation of Homestead / Non-Homestead
		Notice of Penalties for Making False or Misleading Statements
		Ownership Affidavit
		Occupancy and Financial Status Affidavit
		Obligation of Debts Affidavit
		Release of Claims and Hold Harmless Agreement
		Affidavit of Marital Status
		Tax Indemnity
		Compliance / Correction Agreement

Notes:

Ack: Do you acknowledge this as your signature and your free act and deed, for the purposes stated herein?
Jurat: Do you solemnly (swear/affirm) that this statement is true, (so help you God / on your honor)?

| Signer 1 Name and Address: | | Signer 2 Name and Address: | |

Signer 1

Identification Method: ☐ Personally Known ☐ Other
☐ Texas Driver's License ☐ Driver's License ☐ Passport

Signer 2

Identification Method: ☐ Personally Known ☐ Other
☐ Texas Driver's License ☐ Driver's License ☐ Passport

Sign Here

X _____

Sign Here

X _____

Date/Time: _____   Ref#: _____

Signing Address:

Document Date	Notarization Ack Jur Oth Fee if any	Document Description	Signer Initials	
			1	2
		Deed of Trust / Mortgage		
		Deed - General - Quit Claim - Special Warranty		
		Borrower's Title Affidavit		
		Borrower's Closing Affidavit		
		E&O / Compliance Agreement		
		Occupancy Affidavit		
		Signature Name Affidavit		
		Power of Attorney - Limited / Durable		
		T-47 Residential Real Property Affidavit		
		Mineral Rights Acknowledgement and Agreement		

		Designation of Homestead / Non-Homestead
		Notice of Penalties for Making False or Misleading Statements
		Ownership Affidavit
		Occupancy and Financial Status Affidavit
		Obligation of Debts Affidavit
		Release of Claims and Hold Harmless Agreement
		Affidavit of Marital Status
		Tax Indemnity
		Compliance / Correction Agreement

Notes:

191 Ack:Do you acknowledge this as your signature and your free act and deed, for the purposes stated herein?
Jurat: Do you solemnly (swear/affirm) that this statement is true, (so help you God / on your honor)?

| Signer 1 Name and Address: | | Signer 2 Name and Address: | |

Identification Method: ☐ Personally Known ☐ Other
☐ Texas Driver's License ☐ Driver's License ☐ Passport

Identification Method: ☐ Personally Known ☐ Other
☐ Texas Driver's License ☐ Driver's License ☐ Passport

Sign Here

X _____

Sign Here

X _____

Ref#: _____

Date/Time:

Signing Address:

Document Date	Notarization Ack Jur Oth Fee if any	Document Description	Signer Initials	
			1	2
		Deed of Trust / Mortgage		
		Deed - General - Quit Claim - Special Warranty		
		Borrower's Title Affidavit		
		Borrower's Closing Affidavit		
		E&O / Compliance Agreement		
		Occupancy Affidavit		
		Signature Name Affidavit		
		Power of Attorney - Limited / Durable		
		T-47 Residential Real Property Affidavit		
		Mineral Rights Acknowledgement and Agreement		

Designation of Homestead / Non-Homestead																	
Notice of Penalties for Making False or Misleading Statements																	
Ownership Affidavit																	
Occupancy and Financial Status Affidavit																	
Obligation of Debts Affidavit																	
Release of Claims and Hold Harmless Agreement																	
Affidavit of Marital Status																	
Tax Indemnity																	
Compliance / Correction Agreement																	

Notes:

Ack: Do you acknowledge this as your signature and your free act and deed, for the purposes stated herein?
Jurat: Do you solemnly (swear/affirm) that this statement is true, (so help you God / on your honor)?

| Signer 1 Name and Address: | | Signer 2 Name and Address: | |

| Identification Method: ☐ Personally Known ☐ Other | Identification Method: ☐ Personally Known ☐ Other |
| ☐ Texas Driver's License ☐ Driver's License ☐ Passport | ☐ Texas Driver's License ☐ Driver's License ☐ Passport |

Sign Here

Sign Here

X _____

X _____

Date/Time: _____   Ref#: _____

Signing Address: _____

Document Date	Notarization **Ack Jur Oth** Fee if any	Document Description	Signer Initials	
			1	2
		Deed of Trust / Mortgage		
		Deed - General - Quit Claim - Special Warranty		
		Borrower's Title Affidavit		
		Borrower's Closing Affidavit		
		E&O / Compliance Agreement		
		Occupancy Affidavit		
		Signature Name Affidavit		
		Power of Attorney - Limited / Durable		
		T-47 Residential Real Property Affidavit		
		Mineral Rights Acknowledgement and Agreement		

	Designation of Homestead / Non-Homestead
	Notice of Penalties for Making False or Misleading Statements
	Ownership Affidavit
	Occupancy and Financial Status Affidavit
	Obligation of Debts Affidavit
	Release of Claims and Hold Harmless Agreement
	Affidavit of Marital Status
	Tax Indemnity
	Compliance / Correction Agreement

Notes:

195 Ack: Do you acknowledge this as your signature and your free act and deed, for the purposes stated herein?
Jurat: Do you solemnly (swear/affirm) that this statement is true, (so help you God / on your honor)?

| Signer 1 Name and Address: | | Signer 2 Name and Address: | |

Identification Method: ☐ Personally Known ☐ Other
☐ Texas Driver's License ☐ Driver's License ☐ Passport

Identification Method: ☐ Personally Known ☐ Other
☐ Texas Driver's License ☐ Driver's License ☐ Passport

Sign Here

Sign Here

X _____

X _____

Date/Time: _____   Ref#: _____

Signing Address:

Document Date	Notarization Ack Jur Oth Fee if any	Document Description	Signer Initials 1	2
		Deed of Trust / Mortgage		
		Deed - General - Quit Claim - Special Warranty		
		Borrower's Title Affidavit		
		Borrower's Closing Affidavit		
		E&O / Compliance Agreement		
		Occupancy Affidavit		
		Signature Name Affidavit		
		Power of Attorney - Limited / Durable		
		T-47 Residential Real Property Affidavit		
		Mineral Rights Acknowledgement and Agreement		

Designation of Homestead / Non-Homestead															
Notice of Penalties for Making False or Misleading Statements															
Ownership Affidavit															
Occupancy and Financial Status Affidavit															
Obligation of Debts Affidavit															
Release of Claims and Hold Harmless Agreement															
Affidavit of Marital Status															
Tax Indemnity															
Compliance / Correction Agreement															

Notes:

Ack: Do you acknowledge this as your signature and your free act and deed, for the purposes stated herein?
Jurat: Do you solemnly (swear/affirm) that this statement is true, (so help you God / on your honor)?

Signer 1 Name
and Address:

Signer 2 Name
and Address:

Identification Method:☐ Personally Known ☐ Other
☐ Texas Driver's License ☐ Driver's License ☐ Passport

Identification Method:☐ Personally Known ☐ Other
☐ Texas Driver's License ☐ Driver's License ☐ Passport

Sign Here

Sign Here

X _____

X _____

Date/Time: _____   Ref#: _____

Signing Address:

Document Date	Notarization **A**ck **J**ur **O**th Fee if any	Document Description	Signer Initials	
			1	2
		Deed of Trust / Mortgage		
		Deed - General - Quit Claim - Special Warranty		
		Borrower's Title Affidavit		
		Borrower's Closing Affidavit		
		E&O / Compliance Agreement		
		Occupancy Affidavit		
		Signature Name Affidavit		
		Power of Attorney - Limited / Durable		
		T-47 Residential Real Property Affidavit		
		Mineral Rights Acknowledgement and Agreement		

Designation of Homestead / Non-Homestead															
Notice of Penalties for Making False or Misleading Statements															
Ownership Affidavit															
Occupancy and Financial Status Affidavit															
Obligation of Debts Affidavit															
Release of Claims and Hold Harmless Agreement															
Affidavit of Marital Status															
Tax Indemnity															
Compliance / Correction Agreement															

Notes:

199 Ack:Do you acknowledge this as your signature and your free act and deed, for the purposes stated herein?
Jurat: Do you solemnly (swear/affirm) that this statement is true, (so help you God / on your honor)?

Signer 1 Name and Address:		Signer 2 Name and Address:	
Identification Method:☐ Personally Known ☐ Other ☐ Texas Driver's License ☐ Driver's License ☐ Passport		Identification Method:☐ Personally Known ☐ Other ☐ Texas Driver's License ☐ Driver's License ☐ Passport	

Sign Here

X _____

Sign Here

X _____

Date/Time: _____   Ref#: _____

Signing Address:

Document Date	Notarization **A**ck **J**ur **O**th Fee if any	Document Description	Signer Initials	
			1	2
		Deed of Trust / Mortgage		
		Deed - General - Quit Claim - Special Warranty		
		Borrower's Title Affidavit		
		Borrower's Closing Affidavit		
		E&O / Compliance Agreement		
		Occupancy Affidavit		
		Signature Name Affidavit		
		Power of Attorney - Limited / Durable		
		T-47 Residential Real Property Affidavit		
		Mineral Rights Acknowledgement and Agreement		

| | Designation of Homestead / Non-Homestead |
| Notice of Penalties for Making False or Misleading Statements |
| Ownership Affidavit |
| Occupancy and Financial Status Affidavit |
| Obligation of Debts Affidavit |
| Release of Claims and Hold Harmless Agreement |
| Affidavit of Marital Status |
| Tax Indemnity |
| Compliance / Correction Agreement |

Notes:

201 Ack:Do you acknowledge this as your signature and your free act and deed, for the purposes stated herein?
Jurat: Do you solemnly (swear/affirm) that this statement is true, (so help you God / on your honor)?

www.ingramcontent.com/pod-product-compliance
Lightning Source LLC
Chambersburg PA
CBHW071212210326
41597CB00016B/1785